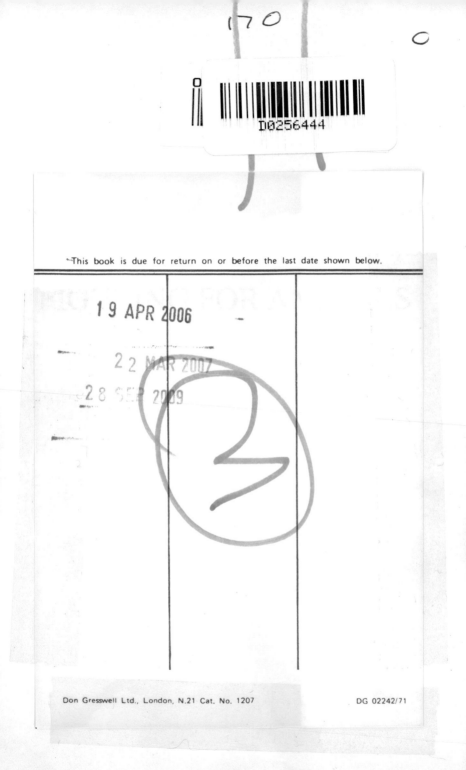

170

0

I0256444

What the papers say about Vernon Coleman and his books:

'Perhaps the best known health writer for the general public in the world today' - The Therapist

'The man is a national treasure' - What Doctors Don't Tell You

'Vernon Coleman writes brilliant books' - The Good Book Guide

'The revered guru of medicine' - Nursing Times

'A literary genius' - HSL Newsletter

'He's the Lone Ranger, Robin Hood and the Equalizer rolled into one' - Glasgow Evening Times

'Britain's leading health care campaigner' - The Sun

'Britain's leading medical author' - The Daily Star

'Brilliant' - The People

'Dr Vernon Coleman is one of our most enlightened, trenchant and sensible dispensers of medical advice' - The Observer

'The patient's champion' - Birmingham Post

'The medical expert you can't ignore' - Sunday Independent

'The most influential medical writer in Britain. There can be little doubt that Vernon Coleman is the people's doctor' - Devon Life

'The doctor who dares to speak his mind' - Oxford Mail

'Man with a mission' - Morning News

'Dr Coleman is more illuminating than the proverbial lady with the lamp' - Company Magazine

'Refreshingly sensible' - Spectator

'Dr Coleman gains in stature with successive books' - Coventry Evening Telegraph

'He writes lucidly and wittily' - Good Housekeeping

'The patient's champion. The doctor with the common touch' - Birmingham Post

'Clear and helpful' - The Guardian

'Vernon Coleman is a leading medical authority and known to millions through his writing, broadcasting and best selling books' - Woman's Own

'His message is important' - The Economist

'It's impossible not to be impressed' - Western Daily Press

'A persuasive writer whose arguments, based on research and experience, are sound' - Nursing Standard

'His book Bodypower' is one of the most sensible treatises on personal survival that has ever been published' - Yorkshire Evening Post

'Dr Coleman is crusading for a more complete awareness of what is good and bad for our bodies. In the course of that he has made many friends and some powerful enemies' - Western Morning News

'His advice is optimistic and enthusiastic' - British Medical Journal

'The calmest voice of reason comes from Dr Vernon Coleman' - The Observer

'A godsend' - Daily Telegraph

A small selection from thousands of readers' letters:

'I admire your forthright and refreshingly honest way of expressing your views and opinions...bless you for being a light in the eternal darkness' - B.O.

'If only more people in the medical profession and this government were like you it would be a much nicer world' - G.W.

'My deep appreciation for your great courage and integrity over the years' - J.T.

'Truly, truly, I greatly admire the work you have done for both animals and man. I think you are wonderful and I wish I had but half your mind power and courage' - A.P.

'I admire your direct approach and philosophy in respect of general health, especially sexual health, environmental and animal issues' A.W.

'It's lovely to have someone who cares about people as you do. You tell us such a lot of things that we are afraid to ask our own doctors' K.C.

'I would like to thank you for telling us the truth' - R.K.

'I feel I must write and congratulate you ... your no-nonsense attitude, teamed with plain common sense makes a refreshing change. Please keep up the good work' - L.B.

'Thanks over and over again - good health always to you as you are fighting for a good cause in life - for the sick' - E.H.

'I only wish to God that we had a few such as your good self in Parliament, then maybe our standard of life would possibly be better' - H.H.

'I must admit that initially I thought that some of your ideas were extreme, but sadly I must concede that I was wrong' - C.D.

'I greatly admire your no nonsense approach to things and your acting as champion of the people' - L.A.

'I have now read and studied all your excellent books and have enjoyed and benefited from them immensely' - B.B.

'May I say that I think you have done a real service to all those who have the sense and patience to study your books' - B.A.

BOOKS BY VERNON COLEMAN

The Medicine Men (1975)
Paper Doctors (1976)
Everything You Want To Know About Ageing (1976)
Stress Control (1978)
The Home Pharmacy (1980)
Aspirin or Ambulance (1980)
Face Values (1981)
Guilt (1982)
The Good Medicine Guide (1982)
Stress And Your Stomach (1983)
Bodypower (1983)
An A to Z Of Women's Problems (1984)
Bodysense (1984)
Taking Care Of Your Skin (1984)
Life Without Tranquillisers (1985)
High Blood Pressure (1985)
Diabetes (1985)
Arthritis (1985)
Eczema and Dermatitis (1985)
The Story Of Medicine (1985)
Natural Pain Control (1986)
Mindpower (1986)
Addicts and Addictions (1986)
Dr Vernon Coleman's Guide To Alternative Medicine (1988)
Stress Management Techniques (1988)
Overcoming Stress (1988)
Know Yourself (1988)
The Health Scandal (1988)
The 20 Minute Health Check (1989)
Sex For Everyone (1989)
Mind Over Body (1989)
Eat Green Lose Weight (1990)
Toxic Stress (1991)
Why Animal Experiments Must Stop (1991)

Books by Vernon Coleman (cont.)

The Drugs Myth (1992)
Why Doctors Do More Harm Than Good (1993)
Stress and Relaxation (1993)
Complete Guide to Sex (1993)
How to Conquer Backache (1993)
How to Conquer Arthritis (1993)
Betrayal of Trust (1994)
Know Your Drugs (1994)
Food for Thought (1994)
The Traditional Home Doctor (1994)
I Hope Your Penis Shrivels Up (1994)
People Watching (1995)
Relief from IBS (1995)
The Parent's Handbook (1995)
Oral Sex: Bad Taste And Hard To Swallow (1995)
Why Is Pubic Hair Curly? (1995)
Men in Dresses (1996)
Power over Cancer (1996)
How To Stop Your Doctor Killing You (1996)
Crossdressing (1996)

novels
The Village Cricket Tour (1990)
The Bilbury Chronicles (1992)
Bilbury Grange (1993)
Mrs Caldicot's Cabbage War (1993)
The Man Who Inherited a Golf Course (1993)
Bilbury Revels (1994)
Deadline (1994)
Bilbury Country (1996)

short stories
Bilbury Pie (1995)

Books by Vernon Coleman (cont.)

on cricket
Thomas Winsden's Cricketing Almanack (1983)
Diary Of A Cricket Lover (1984)

as Edward Vernon
Practice Makes Perfect (1977)
Practise What You Preach (1978)
Getting Into Practice (1979)
Aphrodisiacs - An Owners Manual (1983)
Aphrodisiacs - An Owners Manual (Turbo Edition) (1984)
The Complete Guide To Life (1984)

as Marc Charbonnier
Tunnel (novel 1980)

with Dr Alan C Turin
No More Headaches (1981)

with Alice
Alice's Diary (1989)
Alice's Adventures (1992)

Fighting For Animals

Vernon Coleman

Photographs by Vicky Alhadeff

European Medical Journal

Published in 1996 by the European Medical Journal, Publishing House, Trinity Place, Barnstaple, Devon EX32 9HJ, England

The Questions and Answers in Part Two appeared in Dr Vernon Coleman's column in The People newspaper between December 1992 and May 1996.

Reprinted 2001

ISBN: 1 898947 69 4

A catalogue record of this book is avaliable from the British Library.

Printed and bound by J.W. Arrowsmith Ltd., Bristol

'Truth is on the march and nothing will stop it.'
Emile Zola

CONTENTS

PART ONE

SCREAMS AND NIGHTMARES

'It is only with the heart that one can see rightly; what is essential is invisible to the eye.'
Antoine de Saint Exupéry

1

I will never forget the day I decided that experiments on animals had to be stopped. The experience scarred my memory for life. I was a 19 year old first year medical student - still too ignorant and inexperienced to be allowed out on to the wards. With several of my fellow students I was taken into a physiology laboratory to be taught a little about the human body. The lecturer took a large, frightened-looking cat from an assistant, climbed onto a table, turned the animal on her back and held her high in the air. Then, after ordering us all to watch carefully, he dropped her ten or twelve feet to the ground. The screeching cat landed on her feet and ran off terrified into a corner. I don't know what this experiment was designed to teach us - but I cannot see what relevance it had to the treatment of illness in humans. Already feeling uncomfortable I and a group of students were then ordered to experiment on a live rabbit. I can't remember the details but I do remember that I regarded it as a pointless exercise. I was filled with fury and nausea. How can you learn anything useful about life by torturing and killing, I thought. I couldn't go through with it. Along with several colleagues I walked out of the lab, refusing to have anything more to do with the lesson. As I was leaving, other students began the experiments. The medical establishment must have shared some of my views on the irrelevance of this experiment. No one said anything about my walkout, no one called me back, no one disciplined me. I never completed that particular course - but I qualified as a doctor. This sad experience awakened my curiosity about animal experiments. Secretly, I began to explore the basement which housed the grim cages where cats, rabbits and monkeys were kept. I was sickened by what I saw. I felt the experiments in which these animals would die could have no relevance to humans. I concluded that they could not help me or any one else become a better doctor - and could never help any physician treat patients better. The more I studied the subject, the clearer it became that the anatomical and physiological differences between animals and humans mean animal experiments can never be of practical use to anyone. Animal experiments were done, I decided, because no one cared enough to stop them.

2

Although I also campaign against hunting and all forms of animal cruelty - including the use of animals for food - I am sometimes asked why I've chosen to put so much energy into attacking vivisection rather than other versions of animal cruelty. There are several reasons.

First, vivisection involves huge numbers of animals - around one thousand animals every thirty seconds. That is far, far more than all the forms of hunting, for example. What is more the animals suffer constantly. They are usually kept alone, in tiny cages, until they are used in an experiment. Many are kept alive for months or even years in great distress and pain.

Second, vivisection is probably the best and longest established form of organised, officially acknowledged animal cruelty. It is the one form of animal cruelty for which people have devised spurious but apparently credible excuses. Vivisection is symbolic of the way we treat animals. It has the support of the world's most profitable industries. I believe that when vivisection is banned other forms of animal cruelty will quickly disappear too.

Third, vivisection is the most immoral, academically and intellectually dishonest form of animal abuse. The vivisectionists practice a particularly cruel form of intellectual terrorism: they terrify ordinary people into supporting them by claiming that animal experiments are of medical value. Vivisection affects human beings as well as animals. The vivisectors are responsible for countless human deaths - as well as animal deaths. By stopping vivisection we will also be helping to save human lives and protect human patients.

Now that slavery and apartheid have been abolished I firmly

believe that vivisection is the most evil and barbaric, unjust and un-justifiable practice on earth. We have to stop it. My aim is simple: to stop all animal experiments around the world as soon as possible.

The scientific and medical arguments against vivisection are overwhelming. Morally, there is no question that experimenting on animals is a vile, inexcusable business. Vivisectors will, assuredly, burn in hell for their vile work. Those who oppose animal experimentation are ethically right, morally right and scientifically right.

So why does society allow these scientists to perform these foul experiments?

There are tens of thousands of anti-vivisection groups around the world. Some of these groups have been in existence for a century. Millions of people want animal experiments stopped. So, why is the war against vivisection taking so long to win?

The truth is that animal experiments would have been stopped years ago if the war against vivisection had been better planned and if the anti-vivisection troops had been deployed more effectively. The overpaid vivisectors and their rich supporters ought to have lost decades ago. But they are as clever as they are cruel. They are greedy, manipulative and enormously aggressive.

And we have not fought the war very well so far.

Some organisations prefer a conciliatory approach. They believe that more progress will be made through talking to vivisectors than through confrontation. There is no doubt that these organisations have made progress in persuading laboratories to look after animals better and to search for other ways of doing experiments whenever possible (I try not to use the word 'alternative' because to talk of 'alternatives' suggests that animal experiments have some value).

However, I fear that the truth is that negotiation means compromise. And how can there be any compromise? Those of us who love animals want all animal experiments stopped. The vivisectors want to carry on. And that is that. How can there possibly be any room for negotiation? There is no middle ground.

I have heard anti-vivisectionists claim that they want to stop vivisection from within the system. I don't think that approach will work. No one has ever changed anything from within a system. You can only produce radical changes from outside.

The time has come for a more determined, better-defined attack on vivisection and vivisectors.

I want all animal experiments stopped now. Improving cage sizes or the conditions in which animals are transported and stored is not enough. I fear that if one airline stops carrying animals then another airline will step in. Or the animals will be transported by sea (with journey times being longer).

I have frequently found myself under attack from anti-vivisection groups for my robust and unforgiving attacks on vivisectors. I have seen reports by anti-vivisection groups complaining not about scientists performing animal experiments but about the number of animals they have used - and arguing that the experiments could have been done with fewer animals. I have heard alleged anti-vivisectionists describing abolitionists as the enemy. And I have on many occasions heard anti-vivisection group leaders describing other anti-vivisection groups as 'the competition'. I have even heard anti-vivisectionists arguing that we have to talk with politicians in order to change the laws which force drug companies to perform animal experiments. (There are no laws requiring drug or cosmetic companies to perform animal experiments.)

I fear that those who believe that we can win this battle by negotiation have been conned; seduced by flattery from politicians ('come and have tea with me at the House of Commons and we'll talk about it'). Encouraged to be enthusiastic about the possibility of making small steps towards better conditions (larger cages etc.) they forget that the simple and rational aim is to stop experimentation and they ignore the overpowering evidence in support of that aim. If lobbying was ever going to work it would have worked long ago. I fear that too many anti-vivisectionists no longer believe in their hearts that we can win. They believe that small steps - larger cages, slightly fewer animals, bans on importing animals by air - are all we can hope for.

One anti-vivisectionist told me, rather crossly, 'the vivisectors are not all bad people you know'. Not bad people! These are hateful, cruel, psychopathic beings. These are not people with whom we should have any 'friendly' association. And even to talk about cage sizes and alternatives is to play a dangerous game. Worse still, not believing that we can win is a self fulfilling prophecy. I believe that all these discussions about cage size etc. are initiated by the opposition - who want to keep us distracted from the real argument: abolition. They can keep us going for decades like this (and they have).

The anti-vivisection movement has been in existence for decades. And we have got nowhere. Vivisectors are using as many animals now as they were half a century ago. Battles like ours are never won by negotiation. The suffragettes didn't get the vote through gentle negotiation. Apartheid wasn't smashed by negotiation. Slavery wasn't abolished by quiet, gentlemanly discussions in panelled committee rooms. To win the war against vivisection we must fight our opponents in newspapers and magazines, on radio and television. All we have to do to win is to capture and mobilise public opinion.

3

Many people don't understand exactly what sort of experiments animals are used for. Those who want animal experiments to continue usually argue that the experiments are painless and that the animals do not suffer. The truth is very different. I have filing cabinets filled with research papers from universities and institutions around the world and there seems to be no end to the variety of indignities that researchers can think up for the unfortunate animals in their power. Most of these experiments are performed on your behalf and with your money.

If you are uncertain about the nature of vivisection then try this simple exercise: imagine you are a 'guinea pig' taking part in a sensitisation test for a new perfume.

First, scientists would shave a patch of your skin - removing every small hair - so that the perfume would make the best possible contact with your skin. Then they would put a large quantity of concentrated perfume onto your skin and leave it there. A plaster would be put over the test area to make sure that the perfume remained in the closest possible contact with your skin. You would be tied down to make sure that you didn't move about and disturb the experiment. Every few hours or so the test site would be inspected. And more of the concentrated perfume would be added until your skin went red and started to itch.

You would want to scratch but you wouldn't be able to. A thick dressing would be put over the test area and your hands would be tied to stop you interfering with the experiment. The itching would get worse and worse. But the scientists doing the experiment wouldn't

22

give you anything to stop the itching. If they did they would mess up their results.

Even if you cried and begged for mercy they would ignore you. These scientists are trained to ignore such pleas. It is their job to cause suffering - and to record the consequences.

Gradually, the area of skin under test would become redder and redder. Eventually it would probably begin to blister. Fluids would ooze out of your skin and drip out from underneath your plaster. You would probably notice some blood oozing out as well. Before long your whole body would probably begin to react. You might start to wheeze and to have difficulty in breathing. Your skin would start to burn and to itch and your heart might well start to pound.

The aim of a sensitisation experiment is deliberately to induce an allergy response by giving so much of the test product that the body responds violently. You would feel ill. You would probably feel nauseated and you might start to vomit. Still, the scientists would refuse to give you any treatment in case it interfered with the test. Instead they would simply write down your symptoms and make notes about the condition of your skin. When they had acquired enough information they would kill you.

4

Those who perform and support animal experiments are so embarrassed and ashamed of what they do that they frequently use euphemisms to disguise their activities. It is quite common, for example, for experimenters to talk of animals 'taking part' in experiments and 'helping us with our research'. The word 'experiment' has been replaced by the word 'procedure', which is less evocative. Experimenters have their own language. Here are just a few choice phrases they use (and their meanings):

vocal response = crying

major airway embarrassment = choking

reacting to adverse stimulation with vigorous motor responses = trying to escape

binocular deprivation = sewing the eyes up

decapitation = head removal

exhibiting lethal behaviour = dying

startle reflex = flinching

aversive electrical stimulation = electric shocks

thermal injury = burn or scald

5

'It is dangerous to be right when your government is wrong.'
Voltaire

6

I am constantly saddened (and outraged) by the fact that the official line of many religious leaders is that animals have no rights and are here simply for human beings to do with as they will. A woman with whom I was debating the whole issue of animal experimentation concluded her speech by claiming, as though it was a proven fact, that animals do not have souls and are therefore on earth for humans to use. When I asked her how she knew that animals do not have souls she could not answer. Much formal religion is, it seems to me, more about war, prejudice, smart clothes and extravagant buildings than compassion, love or spiritual integrity.

My god loves all creatures equally. He does not believe that a white man is better than a black man. He does not believe that a black man is better than a red man or a yellow man. He does not believe that a man is better than a woman. He does not believe that a cat is better than a horse or that a horse is better than a dog or a woman. He does not believe that a hippopotamus is better than a mouse or that a mouse is better than a frog or that a frog is better than a man. My god does not believe that a strong man is better than a weak man or that a rich man is better than a poor man. My god loves all creatures equally. I believe that the world would be a happier place if more people were friends with my god.

7

'The great elephant has by nature qualities rarely found in man, namely honesty, prudence, a sense of justice and of religious observance. Consequently, when the moon is new they go down to the rivers and there solemnly cleansing themselves bathe, and after having thus saluted the planet return to the woods. They fear shame and only pair at night and secretly, not do then rejoin the herd but first bathe in the river.'

Leonardo da Vinci

8

Here are nine facts about animal experiments:

1. Every thirty seconds vivisectors kill another thousand animals.

2. Vivisectors use cats, dogs, puppies, kittens, horses, sheep, rats, mice, guinea pigs, rabbits, monkeys, baboons and any other creature you can think of.

3. While waiting to be used in laboratory experiments animals are kept in solitary confinement in small cages. Alone and frightened they can hear the screams of the other animals being used.

4. Many of the animals used in laboratory experiments are 'pets' which have been kidnapped, taken off the streets and sold to the vivisectors.

5. Animals used in experiments are tortured, blinded, burned, shot, injected and dissected. They have their eyes sewn up or their limbs broken. Chemicals are injected into their brains and their screams of anguish are coldly recorded. If the animal lives through this torture it will then be killed.

6. Three quarters of the experiments performed by vivisectors are done without any anaesthetic.

7. Most of the experimenters who torture and kill animals have no medical or veterinary training.

8. Most animal experiments are paid for with your money.

9. Animal experiments are now recognised to be of absolutely no value to patients or doctors or anyone else. Animal experiments are per-

formed by companies wanting to put new products onto the market without doing more expensive tests and by second-rate scientists wanting to acquire academic status the easy way.

9

Think of the animal you love most dearly. If he or she is close to you, reach out and touch him or her. Now, imagine the dog, cat or rabbit you love strapped - alive and alert - to the vivisector's laboratory bench. Imagine the vivisector approaching with scalpel raised. Imagine a tube implanted into the animal's brain and a scientist deliberately injecting an irritating chemical down the tube. Imagine the scientist sitting back and waiting to see what happens. Within a minute or two the animal you love begins to shiver. The shivering is mild at first but it quickly becomes vigorous and widespread. Then the animal begins to cry; loud and pitiful cries. He begins breathing rapidly and salivating. His ears twitch and his hair stands on end. He vomits, wets himself and empties his bowels. The white-coated, cold-blooded scientist who is watching all this dispassionately observes the animal's distress and carefully writes everything down in his notebook.

That is no fiction. It is real. It happens every day. In your name. With your money. And someone else's loved animal. Every 30 seconds that is exactly what happens to 1000 animals. It could happen to your loved animal if the vivisectors get hold of him or her.

10

When official spokesmen speak you should only believe their denials. When official spokesmen deny something you can be confident it is the truth.

11

Uncertainty and change are the greatest cause of stress among people. (It is because of the element of change that moving house is one of the most stressful of all activities). The same is true for animals. So just imagine the emotional trauma animals must feel when they are taken out of their field or barn, herded into a cramped truck and driven for hour after hour after hour to where they know not.

12

Nobody does what they don't want to do.

13

The European Union has rules to protect animals while they are being transported. The rules say that animals must be fed and watered after travelling for 24 hours. Hands up those who would like to see EU bureaucrats travelling across Europe under those conditions.

14

Walking by the river I paused to remonstrate gently with a fisherman. A trout he had caught was lying on the bank, thrashing around. I moved forwards to try and pick up the fish so that I could throw it back into the water. But I was too far away. The fisherman saw me, reached out, picked up the fish by its tail and killed it by banging its head on a rock. When I tried to explain to the fisherman that he was indulging in a cruel sport he turned round and started hurling abuse at me. He told me to go away and stop disturbing the fish. As I walked away he threw a stone at me. It missed. He then threw several more stones in my direction. The stones did not hit me - partly because the fisherman was a rather poor shot and partly because I kept ducking and weaving - but there is absolutely no doubt that they were aimed directly at me.

When I got to the nearest village I telephoned the police to complain.

They were not interested in my complaint and refused to do anything.

Can it be that throwing stones is no longer a crime? I wonder what would have happened if an animal rights campaigner had thrown stones at a fisherman, a hunter or a lorry driver transporting calves or lambs to a bloody death. Am I unfair in suspecting that the police might have responded differently?

15

The mad cow scandal should have awakened us all to the fact that most farmers - like the rest of the huge army of slimy good for nothings involved in the dead animal business - are pustulant, crooked, self centred, stupid, greedy bastards concerned only with their own profits.

But the eternally damned farmers are so skilful at manipulating politicians and the media that they actually managed to make most people feel sorry for them!

The farmers, the butchers and the abattoir workers have all bleated about financial losses, redundancies and bleak futures.

But the fact is that for years now farmers and others involved in the meat business have been taking risks with the lives of those who buy their products simply so that they could make more money.

It was the farmers - manipulative money grubbers that they are - who chose to feed their animals the food which created the problem.

Years ago those in the animal murdering business could have protected themselves - and the meat eating world - from the horrors of Mad Cow Disease. They could have taken tougher, stricter action ages ago. But they didn't. They - and the British government - insisted that there wasn't a problem.

Even if they didn't know for certain that there was a problem coming (and I think they should have known) they should have realised that there was a big risk.

Now, what would happen if any other businessman cut corners, took risks with the customers' lives and caused panic and chaos?

Would he expect his customers to pay for all his losses and give him compensation to make sure that he didn't lose any money? Or would he start looking for a sharp lawyer to protect him against the lawsuits that he knew would soon start thudding on his doorstep?

So, why were are you and I expected to fork out our hard-earned cash to pay for this greed-inspired error?

The truth is that the Mad Cow disease scandal is just one example of the many ways in which farmers have for decades recklessly exposed ordinary people to danger.

I believe it was the overuse of antibiotics - given to animals to keep them 'healthy' and therefore increase profits - which helped create a world in which infections are now rapidly increasing.

Every time you read about a hospital infection which cannot be controlled by antibiotics I think you should remember the farmers.

I also believe that the reckless use of other drugs and hormones has contaminated farm products for decades. The over use of fertilisers, pesticides and other chemicals has polluted our water supplies and poisoned thousands of consumers.

Today farmers are messing around with genetically manipulated animals and crops because they see more ways to increase their profits. They don't give a damn that they are playing a dangerous game and that they are likely to produce permanent and terrifying changes in our world.

The farmers don't give a fig for your health or your children's health. All they care about is profits.

(Somehow, to add to all this, the farmers even manage to persuade politicians to give them subsidies! Daft as it may sound it's all a bit like murderers and poisoners demanding - and getting - financial help!)

The worst thing is that the politicians who are hired and paid to protect us don't give a damn about what the farmers do either.

They just let them get on with it.

The only ray of hope in this whole sad and sorry mess is that more and more people may now stop eating beef - and other types of meat.

Through their ignorance, their stupidity and their greed the meat farmers might just have helped to put themselves out of business.

I do hope so.

The evidence now shows clearly that meat can cause cancer and can be a major factor in the development of heart disease.

Mass bankruptcy among farmers, butchers and others involved in the animal-murdering business is a joyful thought.

16

A friend in Australia sent me a newspaper cutting. The article on the clipping described how a rich man is putting fences around huge areas of land, killing the feral animals within the fences and then installing animals from endangered species. I totally disapprove. This killing is, it seems to me, being done for the sake of humans. It may be nice for us to be able to see lots of different species of animals. But it is of no concern to the animals involved. If a species dies out then it dies out. To kill animals so that you can save other animals is wrong.

17

We can learn so much from animals. Why, oh why, do our scientists insist on cutting up animals, ripping out their organs, injecting them with noxious chemicals and subjecting them to endless tortures when they could learn far, far more simply by observing them? If architecture students wandered around the world knocking down cathedrals, palaces and other structural works of art - and then excused themselves by saying that they wanted to know more about how these buildings were constructed we would describe them as wicked philistines. If a man in a white coat said that he was knocking down the Notre Dame in Paris because he thought it would help him design a suspension bridge or repair a mediaeval thatched cottage we would think him completely mad.

We can learn much from animals - but by observing them not from torturing and killing them.

18

'If your happiness depends on what somebody else does,' wrote Richard Bach in *Illusions*, 'I guess you do have a problem.'

All those who love animals, and feel strongly about the way in which they are mistreated, will know what he meant.

In my book *Toxic Stress* I argued that many of the most potent, destructive and stressful forces in our society are outside our personal control; they are a result of our living in a sophisticated and so called civilised community. These external stresses, ones which cannot be alleviated by learning how to deal with stress or by making an effort to live a less stressful life, are most damaging because the frustration, anger and sense of impotence they produce cannot be countered by any logical means.

Most of my personal concerns and anxieties and pains are provoked by worries which are of no direct concern to me. This adds an extra dimension to the concept of 'toxic stress'. The fact that the most frustrating and exhausting anxieties in my life do not directly concern me and are generated by parts of society which are outside my control makes them doubly stressful.

One of the great injustices of this life is that those who are compassionate and who care suffer for the crimes of those who are neither compassionate nor who care. The hunter does not suffer any pangs of conscience and neither does the vivisector. The caring, compassionate human being suffers on their behalf.

19

'Is it not a reproach that man is a carnivorous animal? True, he can and does live, in a great measure, by preying on other animals; but this is a miserable way - as any one who will go to snaring rabbits, or slaughtering lambs, may learn - and he will be regarded as a benefactor of his race who shall teach man to confine himself to a more innocent and wholesome diet. Whatever my own practice may be, I have no doubt that it is a part of the destiny of the human race, in its gradual improvement, to leave off eating animals, as surely as the savage tribes have left off eating each other when they came in contact with the more civilised.'
Henry David Thoreau

20

When you and I see an animal we look, we watch, we admire, we respect and we maybe even love. When the vivisector sees an animal he sees an object; a piece of scientific material. He thinks: 'I would like to cut up that creature.'

Maybe, I thought at first, the vivisector does not understand the wickedness of what he does because the people around him are all involved too. But that is no answer. A man or woman with a conscience could not possibly approve of vivisection. It is as foul a trade as was ever invented by man.

Torturing and then killing cats, kittens, dogs, puppies, mice, guinea pigs, rats, monkeys, hamsters, rabbits and other animals is morally indefensible, ethically inexcusable, and medically and scientifically unsustainable.

The things vivisectors do to animals are so awful, so disgusting that I dare not describe them in newspaper articles or columns. Readers would, I know, be so sickened that they would simply turn over the page.

I am, in my heart, convinced that all those who practise vivisection are psychopaths; unfeeling, unthinking, unseeing; blind to all that is good and with minds open only to the possibility of personal and professional gain, however it may be obtained.

It is my professional medical opinion that the thousands of vivisectors who do the torturing and the killing must have the same sort of general psychological make up as serial killers. They must be deeply sick to be able to inflict pain on animals for day after day. They are, I rather suspect, the sort of cruel individuals who obtained pleasure from pulling the wings off flies and shooting birds with airguns when they were small.

Vivisectors around the world sometimes claim that their experiments are of value to doctors. They try to excuse their foul and barbaric deeds by claiming that the work they do saves lives. I believe that is a lie. And I believe that the vivisectionists know that it is a lie.

I have frequently challenged vivisectors and their supporters to debate their foul work with me on national TV or radio. But these days they are too cowardly; too afraid to risk being exposed for the pseudo-scientific charlatans they are.

The truth is that we would all be much, much better off if vivisection had never been invented. (When it is stopped it will never be started again.) I believe that animal experiments are done because they enable drug companies to get new products onto the market quickly and easily.

It is, I think, a cynical and cruel business.

I believe that animal experimentation is one of the reasons why four out of ten patients who receive drugs suffer side effects.

And it is, I believe, partly because drug companies are allowed to rely so much on animal experiments that one in six individuals in hospital are there because they have been made ill by a doctor.

I don't think any animal experiments save human lives. On the contrary, I believe that men, women and children suffer agonies - and die - because of animal experiments.

Every night, when you go to bed, ask yourself: 'What have I

done today to help stop animal experiments.'

You will, I suspect, find that you will sleep easier if you have done something to help stop vivisection.

21

Scientists are now using vast numbers of animals in experiments designed to help them look for ways to treat a wide variety of diseases including narrowed arteries, heart disease, high blood pressure, stroke and other cardiovascular disorders which so often result in early deaths.

But we already know what causes most cases of heart disease, high blood pressure, stroke and other cardiovascular calamities.

The individual who wants to avoid these disorders can best do so by avoiding fatty food and tobacco, minimising his exposure to stress (or enhancing his ability to deal with it) and taking regular, gentle exercise. Like cancer, heart disease is, to a remarkably large extent, a disease of choice.

Sadly, however, I fear that simple preventive medicine is of very little interest to scientists. How can the expenditure of billions of dollars on laboratories, white coated scientists and animal houses be justified when the solutions are so simple?

The scientists have to keep searching for more complex solutions because they, and their masters at the drug companies, cannot make a living out of teaching people how to avoid disease.

The drug companies (which pay for much of the world's research) want complex, pharmacological solutions because they know that their profits will only be enhanced when they can offer consumers pills for all their ills.

And the drug companies are comforted by the knowledge that the average citizen is not willing to make even the slightest effort on his own behalf to maintain, sustain or restore his health. He would much rather take a pill (however expensive it might be and however hazardous the consequences might be) than change his diet or take a long term, personal approach to his health and his life. He would rather hand over responsibility to people he does not know and will never meet, and who regard him solely as a source of profit, rather than take responsibility for his own health.

22

Has anyone else noticed that experiments done on animals seem to be ignored if the results are commercially or politically embarrassing or inconvenient? In my book *Betrayal of Trust* I named around fifty prescription drugs which are considered perfectly safe for human use - but which can all cause cancer and other serious health problems when given to animals.

23

'You have just dined and however scrupulously the slaughterhouse is concealed in the graceful distance of miles, there is complicity.'
Ralph Waldo Emerson

24

The refusal of most editors and producers either to take on the meat industry or to promote anything which might be seen as sympathetic towards animals has been illustrated painfully vividly by the fact that my book *Power over Cancer* has been almost totally ignored by newspapers, magazines, TV stations and radio stations.

The book explains how it is possible to avoid 80% of all cancers by avoiding fatty foods and meat products and by eating a healthy mixture of the right vegetables, fruit and grains. I included in the book excerpts from no less than 26 scientific papers which provide evidence illustrating the link between meat and fat and cancer. Details of *Power over Cancer* were sent to hundreds of editors and producers but so far, very few publications have even mentioned the book.

I am genuinely surprised and saddened. I would have thought that even if editors had decided to attack the book's existence they would have found it difficult to ignore the claims I make (all of which I can justify). For example, the press release pointed out that many of the women who died of breast cancer last year could still be alive today if they had read *Power over Cancer*. If the claim is false then I should be attacked. If the claim is true then how can it be ignored?

The failure of the media even to discuss this subject depresses me enormously. How can editors and producers ignore a book which could save tens of thousands of lives a year in Britain alone? Every week I am invited to appear on television or radio programmes to talk about issues about which I know little and care nothing. (I always say 'No'). And yet this vitally important issue is ignored.

Part of the problem is that no one wants to write or speak about cancer. The very word itself is 'taboo'.

Part of the problem is that the meat industry is too rich and too powerful to annoy.

And part of the problem is that many editors and producers would undoubtedly regard *Power over Cancer* as an 'animal rights' book. And the editors who work on broadsheet newspapers and the producers who work on television and radio programmes hardly ever take a sympathetic line towards animal rights issues. Indeed, they usually lean very heavily on the side of those who want to continue to do pointless and barbaric things to animals.

The following short extract comes from one of the few reviews of Power over Cancer to appear in any publication - it was published in a local newspaper:

'The Sun's doctor offers advice on how to cut your cancer risk by 80 per cent. I find this quite frightening if people are going to read this and believe they will avoid cancer.'

I wrote to the Editor of the publication concerned and pointed out that I had not been a columnist on The Sun newspaper for four years. I also pointed out that I had filled the book with scientific evidence in support of my claim.

I did not receive a reply. And as far as I am aware my letter was not published.

Three months later the same publication printed a review of my book *How To Stop Your Doctor Killing You.*

The reviewer wrote:

'I'm sorry. I realise Dr Vern is a bit of a national hero to readers of the Sun, but I don't trust him.'

'This book proves it. It aims to undermine the professionals who have spent years learning the business.'

'Sure some people make mistakes, but to question the experts every step of the way is a little insulting to say the least.'

In the book I point out that one in six patients in hospital are there because they have been made ill by a doctor. I find it alarming to think that there are people around who feel that 'to question the experts every step of the way is a little insulting to say the least'.

25

I read today that one of America's most horrific mass murderers (a man who is infamous for having eaten the dead bodies of his victims) used to do foul things to animals when he was a boy. I am not surprised. I am convinced that people who can do cruel things to animals can do equally cruel things to other human beings. The boy who shoots cats and birds will grow up to be a vivisector, a brutal police officer or a mass murderer.

26

All over the world smokers who have developed cancer or other diseases after smoking cigarettes are suing tobacco companies. I don't entirely understand the logic of these lawsuits. Surely individuals who chose to smoke knew the risk they were taking? I have little doubt that in a few years time meat eaters who have developed cancer will sue butchers and others in the meat industry. But anyone who eats meat today has chosen their own destiny. If they develop cancer they have no one to blame but themselves.

27

Someone sent me a cutting today in which a vivisectionist complained that anti-vivisectionists invariably refuse to engage in debate! The writer of this piece complained that anti-vivisectionists are part of the anti-intellectual fringe of our society. What amazing lies these people tell. And what heights of self delusion they reach. Vivisectionists often seem to regard themselves as intellectuals. What nonsense. These people are intellectual froth; all bubbles and no substance. And as for their claim that anti-vivisectionists refuse to debate the issue - the exact opposite is the truth!

I was invited some time ago to speak at a large university in a debate about vivisection. The invitation was withdrawn when the organisers could not find anyone prepared to debate with me. I offered to do both sides of the debate but the organisers did not seem too keen on this suggestion. (I am told that the debate eventually went ahead - without me.)

28

A diet which contains plenty of meat and fat is unhealthy. Meat causes cancer. Fat causes cancer and heart disease.

Add the risks of mad cow disease to cancer and heart disease and it isn't difficult to see why a harmburger is the culinary equivalent of an anti-personnel mine. If Lucretia Borgia were alive and cooking she would love harmburgers.

Intelligent people in developed countries who want to stay healthier and live longer are reducing their intake of these killer foods.

But farmers and the food industry are fighting hard to keep their profits high - whatever the cost to the rest of the world may be.

Not content with having wrecked the health of several generations of citizens in the so called developed countries of the west, these ruthless profiteers - unable to sell their deadly wares to the better informed citizens of the west - are now making a determined effort to start selling their cancerous, artery clogging fare to citizens in the developing countries of the world.

As a result, millions of members of China's new middle class are now turning away from traditional rice and vegetable dishes (the sort of foods now recognised as healthy and favoured by intelligent eaters in the west) and stuffing themselves with meat laden old style western dishes. In their gentle, oriental innocence they presumably believe that harmburgers and other killer foods are good for them. There is more than a little irony in the fact that as the developed west turns vegetarian so the developing countries are eating more meat.

All around the world, as disposable incomes rise, millions of people start eating meat - and, sadly and misguidedly, think they are eating better! Steakhouses and harmburger outlets are springing up all over the world and the consumption of pork, lamb, beef and chicken is increasing rapidly in countries which, until a year or two ago, regarded such foods as bizarre luxuries. The global consumption of beef, poultry and pork has gone up 11% in the last year. Even though the informed and intelligent consumer in the west is eating less meat the consumption of beef, pork, poultry and mutton around the world has been rising for a quarter of a century.

The result of this mass marketing of death foods is, of course, entirely predictable: within a decade or two the incidence of heart disease and cancer in China and other developing countries will start to rocket.

The food industry will have sustained its profits by successfully exporting cancer and heart disease to the emerging nations of the world.

But the malign influence of the farmers and the food industry will affect more than morbidity and mortality rates in developing countries: the consequences of this latest exhibition of the power of greed over sense will not be confined to far away hospitals and distant mortuaries but will affect every one of us.

The first and most obvious problem is the fact that food production is inefficient when animals are involved. One hundred acres of land will produce enough wheat to feed 240 people but only enough beef for 20 people. Pigs have to be fed four kilograms of grain if they are to produce one kilogram of pork. Half the rainforests in the world have already been destroyed to clear ground to graze cattle to make beefburgers.

And the inevitable result is there are going to be even greater world wide shortages of grains.

The worldwide surge in the prices of grains in the mid 1990s was no accident: it was the direct result of the increase in the consumption of meat in developing countries. Every time another harmburger bar opens the amount of grain available to feed starving millions drops appreciably. The grain is used to feed cattle or pigs and the quantity of food available for human consumption shrinks. The price of wheat, corn and soyabean will soar and even less food will be available for the starving millions. In Africa and Asia the new middle classes are eating meat today and the poor are even less likely to eat at all tomorrow.

As I write there are 800 million malnourished people in the world. By next week the figure will be higher.

There is plenty of food in the world to feed the 800 million but the food industry wastes what is available by turning nutritious, healthy grains and vegetables into far more profitable meat and meat products.

All this hides another, more sinister danger.

In an attempt to keep up with the world's distorted requirements for food, scientists and farmers are busy messing around with genes in an attempt to grow bigger crops.

Modern, laboratory bred crops help boost yields and profits.

But there is a risk because new crop varieties are identical: each ear of wheat, each potato, each tomato is the same as the one next to it. And each farmer grows the same crop variety in order to maximise his profits.

This is all very well when everything goes fine.

But when a bug comes along which affects one plant every plant will be affected.

And the result will be a wipeout.

About 150 years ago a fungus caused the Irish potato famine.

Today, we are far more vulnerable than the Irish were.

One new fungus or other infection which affects the latest laboratory engineered crop could cause a worldwide shortage of wheat or potatoes and a worldwide famine.

I have no doubt that it will happen soon.

And when it does the farmers whose crops have been destroyed will demand cash so that they don't suffer financially.

No one in the food industry will give a damn about the fact that deaths from starvation will rocket - as a direct result of their greedy, selfish, short sighted policies.

Thanks to the farmers and the food industry the long term future for the world is hunger, growing food shortages and wars as the starving fight for food.

29

An anti-vivisection group told me off for writing a blistering article about vivisection. 'We are not in the business of embarrassing vivisectors,' a spokesman told me. Maybe they should be.

30

What a tragedy it is that so very few people are prepared to stand up and make their voices heard. I receive many, many letters from readers who tell me that they support the things I say about the abuse of animals but that they dare not do anything or speak out because they are too frightened. Most people seem to fear that they will be ridiculed by their friends, relatives and neighbours. Some are frightened that their jobs may be at risk. I can understand their fear - I have been fired many times for being too outspoken. But without public support we will never win. And silence does not help the animals.

31

The vivisection battle is truly one-sided. Those of us who fight vivisection do so at our own expense. We either use our own resources to pay for our campaigns or we raise money for stamps and leaflet printing in pennies. Those who fight for vivisection do so with big money behind them.

32

My sympathies are entirely with those who want the live exports of animals to stop. It is clearly wrong that animals should be cooped up in lorries, without food or water, for hours and hours and even days at a time. Animals do not like being soaked in one another's urine and covered in one another's faeces. They suffer from hunger just like you and I do. They suffer fear just as you and I do. (It occurs to me that the adrenalin levels in these animals must be sky high when they are finally killed. Just what that does to the people who eat them I cannot imagine.)

But I do not feel that a ban on animal exports goes anywhere near far enough. I want to see all cruelty to animals stopped. And this means completely stopping the meat trade - not just the export of live animals.

I believe that one of the best ways to persuade people to stop eating animals is to teach them that animals are sensitive, understanding, compassionate and thoughtful creatures.

When people understand that the steak or chop on their plate is hacked from a living, thinking being then they will, perhaps, stop eating animals. Maybe, eventually, they will regard eating animals as just as barbaric a practice as eating people.

33

Our society sneers at and scorns the unusual or the eccentric. Politicians are frightened of anything new or challenging. They reject the innovative, the creative and the imaginative in favour of the accustomed, the comfortable and the ordinary. It will not, I fear, be long before mediocrity and incompetence are regarded as essential virtues; the necessary building blocks for personal and professional success. In schools mediocrity will be taught as a social necessity; compulsory for commercial or personal success. Creativity will be regarded as politically incorrect and therefore unacceptable. Originality will be suffocated.

The danger now is that the great thinkers of tomorrow will never even develop - let alone survive or thrive to find themselves struggling against the eternally powerful barriers erected by the establishment of the day.

This is a tragedy of monumental proportions for the lone eccentric voice, speaking out against perceived wisdom, is often right and the experts and the officials are often wrong.

If the politically correct have their way and the social workers and bureaucrats take over the world there will be no place in the 21st century for great thinkers and leaders like Christ, Paracelsus, Galileo, Confucius or Socrates.

The future will lie firmly in the hands of the mediocre and the incompetent.

34

'No humane being, past the thoughtless age of boyhood, will wantonly murder any creature, which holds its life by the same tenure that he does. The hare in its extremities cries like a child.'
Henry David Thoreau

35

'If it's the health of my kid or the lives of a thousand cats and dogs then the dogs and cats have to be sacrificed,' said one young father I know, defending vivisection.

'Why would scientists do animal experiments if they weren't useful?' demanded his wife. 'I don't want to know what they do,' she added quickly. 'But I'm sure they wouldn't do what they do if it wasn't necessary.'

Those who believe that animal experiments are useful exhibit a rather pathetic mixture of ignorance and naiveté. They don't want to know the facts because the facts - that millions of animals are tortured and killed with our money purely for commercial profit - are too awful to contemplate.

36

A book buyer who had purchased a copy of my book *Food for Thought* rang the office to congratulate us on updating and reprinting the book so quickly. The member of staff who took the call was puzzled. *Food for Thought* has been reprinted many times but it has not yet been necessary to update it. She asked the caller what she meant. The caller explained that she was very impressed with the updated section referring to the link between eating beef and the human equivalent of Mad Cow Disease. The member of staff explained that the section had been in the book, unaltered, since the book was first published in 1994 (though I had written it in 1992).

I wonder if there is anyone in the country stupid enough to believe what any politician tells them about Mad Cow Disease (or anything else for that matter). I suspect that anyone who still eats beef must be so dotty that doctors won't be able to tell the difference if they do develop Mad Cow Disease.

I first warned about the dangers of eating beef early in May 1990 when I was, I believe, the first doctor in the world to issue a public warning. I was, naturally, widely vilified by medical experts and journalists alike.

'Mad Cow Disease could be the biggest threat to human health since the Black Death plague that killed millions in Europe in the 14th century,' I said in 1990. 'There is already evidence to show that Mad Cow Disease is a bigger threat to humans than AIDS ever was.'

As always I based my view on sound evidence. There was plenty of research to convince me that the disease could spread from species to species - and that it could affect human beings. I warned that it would take several years for the problem to develop - and pleaded with the government to take action.

I have repeated my warning on numerous occasions.

On March 14th 1993 I warned that 'Mad Cow Disease' could be the biggest killer of the century.

'Don't eat beef, hamburgers or anything made from beef,' I warned. 'If you do, I believe you could be taking a real risk.'

The British government's Chief Medical Officer, Dr Kenneth Calman reassured meat eaters that beef could safely be eaten by everyone - children as well as adults.

'To say that Dr Coleman's views are alarmist would be an understatement' announced Dr Calman.

Over twenty years ago I warned that doctors were over prescribing antibiotics. I was laughed at. I warned that screening programmes were ineffective, costly and potentially dangerous. I was scorned. Now who disagrees with me?

Fifteen years ago I warned that hormones in our drinking water were endangering male fertility. I was described as a lunatic. My warnings about the spread of tuberculosis and the dangers of violence on TV were both ignored too.

Ten years ago I warned that electrical appliances could cause cancer. I advised parents to keep children at a distance from TV sets. Politicians and doctors said I was crazy. But now more and more experts agree with me.

Years ago my warnings about vaccines aroused violent and often personal attacks. My warnings about the health risks of passive smoking were ignored for years.

I first warned about the dangers associated with tranquillisers back in 1973. For years I was attacked, derided and scoffed at by politicians and doctors. In 1988 the British government admitted that I was right - tranquillisers could be addictive. Doctors were given an official warning - and the British government publicly stated that they had given the official warning because of my articles.

But I had been giving the same warnings for 15 years!

When I recently published evidence showing a link between meat and cancer politicians and the medical establishment ignored my warnings.

I have frequently been accused of exaggerating health risks to make a good story.

But way back in the 1980s, when just about every doctor, politician and journalist in the country was screaming about the dangers of AIDS, I pointed out that the available scientific evidence clearly showed that AIDS was not a major threat to heterosexuals. I was widely vilified for telling the truth.

I have consistently been threatened, harassed and lied about.

I believe that the government has for years been frightened to admit that Mad Cow Disease was a major threat. Farmers and the meat industry are very powerful.

I don't much care any more when politicians lie to save their own skins. I don't think people expect politicians to be honest. And they know that if one lot is forced to resign another set of greasy contemptibles will take over.

But I do object when politicians fail to tell doctors and the public the whole truth about health matters. And I object too when the government seems to put business above health.

37

Today I read again a claim that animals do not have souls. How can anyone make such a claim? How can any man or woman have the arrogance to decide to which creatures god has, or has not, chosen to give souls? (But do vivisectors have souls, I wonder?)

38

An interviewer said to me today that she thought that my newspaper column might be an embarrassment to those who love animals and object to the use of animals in experiments. She pointed out that in a recent edition of the column I had sandwiched a reply expressing my distaste for vivisection in between two replies responding to questions

44

about sexual and social behaviour. She asked me if I did not feel that it was inappropriate to place a comment about animal experimentation in between such topics. I pointed out that the column has well over six million readers in the U.K. alone, and that without the light-hearted answers and the irrelevant nonsense with which my column is studded, I would have far fewer readers. I argued that in my view the impact of the material about animals is greater because of the circumstances in which it is placed. And I pointed out that since I was originally hired to write an agony column - dealing with psychological and sexual problems - it was, if anything, the question on animal experimentation which was out of place.

Nevertheless, such criticisms are commonplace. I regularly receive letters from animal rights supporters who think that my tabloid newspaper column is a disgrace because it contains questions and answers which do not deal with animal rights. I wonder how many of these people ignore their own employers' requirements and spend the time when they are supposed to be 'working' campaigning against animal cruelty? Although I have resigned from writing that particular column I wonder how many other anti-vivisectionists have been able regularly to reach an audience of millions?

39

I regularly receive a small amount of mail from people who support animal experimentation. Most of them use green ink and write their correspondence in large, capital letters. Sometimes they build up their letters with individual words cut out of newspapers and magazines.

This letter came today.

'You will die. Why you love animals is stupid? Your sick. I am going to kill you and youre animals. I hate animals. They are all messy and stupid. I think their should be more experiment. Animals is just their for people to use.'

This was, I think, the most cogently argued supporting argument for vivisection that I have ever seen. This letter clearly came from one of the most intellectually astute vivisectionists.

40

I receive as many angry letters from people claiming to be animal rights supporters as I do from vivisection supporters. There are letters from people who have been told that I am not medically qualified, that I support violence, that I have been struck off the medical register and all sorts of other fictions. I have even been attacked for writing and promoting my books to a popular audience. These people, who claim to oppose animal cruelty, usually write to tell me that they think I am a disgrace to the animal rights movement and that they do not want to be associated in any way with me. Some of the letters are cruelly personal. I wonder if they also find the time to write letters protesting about hunting, vivisection and other aspects of animal cruelty?

41

I have had files stolen from my home. Attempts have repeatedly been made to burgle my offices. People who work for me have suffered mysterious burglaries during which nothing was taken. Promotions planned for my books have suddenly, and mysteriously, been abandoned. Entirely false rumours have been spread about me. My telephone has suddenly stopped working just before I have been due to broadcast. And messages have been mysteriously sucked off my telephone answering machine. Strangers have knocked on my door, asked me to confirm that I am me, stared at me for a few moments and then walked away. Private detectives have followed my movements. Papers have been stolen from my jacket - and my wallet left behind. It would be easy to become paranoid.

42

When I was eighteen I worked for eight months as a full-time voluntary worker in the North of England. I had just left school and had decided to take a year off before going to medical school. It was a raw part of the world where there was much violence, despair and misery. My job was to act as a catalyst - to encourage local young people to get involved in helping their own community. For example, I went round all the schools and youth clubs and factories recruiting young people to help decorate old people's flats and provide other simple services. I then went door to door finding out who needed help with their home or garden. I don't know why I did this but in order to encourage the kids to help I told them that it would be fun. I warned them that what they would be doing might get them into trouble since we did not have permission to do all this work. (This claim quickly proved to be true: our combined efforts very nearly led to problems when workmen discovered that a small army of young people was doing work which should have been done by them.)

At the end of the eight months I spoke at a conference of voluntary workers. The hall where I spoke was full of people who were doing good works. In my short speech I said that in my experience people who did things for other people, or who tried to improve the world, did so partly for selfish reasons. I pointed out that the kids who had joined my gang of painters and decorators and gardeners had, in my view, not done so because they wanted to help old people whom they didn't even know but partly because the whole project sounded like fun and partly because it was against the rules.

Most of the people in the hall were shocked. I was told that I should not judge other peoples motives by my own. The implication was clear: voluntary workers do what they do out of a sense of spiritual goodness and not for anything they can get of what they do.

Thirty odd years on I am convinced that I was right. People who do things for others - or to improve the world - do so for selfish reasons. There is nothing at all wrong with that. The reasons don't matter a damn. But it is a fact of life.

I spent much of my earlier life campaigning for people. I now spend much of my time campaigning for animals. These campaigns were and are inspired by the fact that I feel anger, sadness and frustration at the way people and animals are treated by our world. I have to do something to help counter the cruelty and the injustice or else the anger and the frustration will eat me away. I have to turn my sadness into anger and my anger into action.

I hope that people and animals benefit from my campaigns but that doesn't alter the fact that what I am doing is also for me.

And the same is, I believe, true of everyone else who campaigns against cruelty or injustice.

43

An anonymous letter came from a reader who wanted me to expose something his or her company is doing which he or she regards as immoral, unethical and cruel to animals. He or she insists that I cannot use his or her name or any of the information included in the letter (there wasn't much, but what there was seemed pretty damning). There are no names or addresses so I cannot check out any of the information myself. The anonymous letter writer explains that if he or she is identified he or she may lose his or her job. Why do so few people have any courage? What miserable existences they lead. So few people are prepared to put their heads above the parapet. But they all seem happy for me to take all the risks for them. Sadly, I cannot do anything with the information which I was sent because I cannot go into print without evidence.

44

What sort of person could work as a vivisector or abattoir worker - hearing, ignoring and working through the screams of animals every day? And what sort of person could possibly marry or live with a vivisector or abattoir worker? The relatives of these evil people must be constantly ashamed. I wonder if the incidence of mental illness and depression is greater among the relatives of vivisectors and abattoir workers? If not then the only answer must be that vivisectors and abattoir workers (and others in similar employment) must attract and develop 'relationships' with psychopathic individuals.

45

I have heard vivisectors arguing that because animals are sometimes cruel to one another it is perfectly all right for human beings to treat animals cruelly. This seems to me to be a very poor argument - even for vivisectors. It is rather like arguing that World War II concentration camp guards were cruel to human beings and so it is perfectly all right for all of us to be cruel to one another.

    We are supposed to be a superior species; and yet we are far crueller than any other species.

46

It seems to me that the majority of 'broadsheet' newspapers (the ones which regard themselves as 'intellectual' and which have been described as the 'unpopular press' in contrast to the tabloid 'popular press') are in favour of vivisection. I cannot remember ever having seen an article in broadsheet newspaper attacking vivisection.

Writing for the 'broadsheet' newspapers is very easy. I wrote for The Guardian when I was in my teens and I contributed regularly to the other major broadsheet newspapers during my twenties. I suspect that the broadsheets take this pro-vivisection stance because the journalists who work for them these days are of rather inferior intellectual quality and are greatly influenced by the minor academics who favour animal experimentation. There is much friendship between these two groups. The journalists are flattered to be able to associate with the academics and the academics are delighted to be able to use the pages of the broadsheet newspapers to defend their evil work. The tabloid newspapers are much more inclined to publish articles attacking vivisection and much braver and much more courageous about attacking or challenging the scientific and medical establishments.

47

I met a doctor who is a vegetarian. He told me that his colleagues all regard him as a lunatic. He genuinely believes that his vegetarianism has had an adverse effect on his career. He says he is pointed to and laughed at when he goes to medical meetings. Other doctors make lots of weak jokes about lentils and lettuce. He says he particularly dislikes the colleagues who feign concern for his health and ask him what vitamin and mineral supplements he takes. He is, he told me, surprised at the level of ignorance about nutrition among members of the medical profession. I told him that although I was sad I wasn't in the slightest bit surprised to hear about the way he is treated. I told him that I had recently received a letter from a girl who complained that when she visited her doctor she noticed that her computerised medical notes contained the words 'Inadequate Diet'. The doctor admitted that this referred to the fact that she is a vegetarian. Even more worrying is the fact that the phrase had not been put into the computer by the girl's doctor but that it was part of the software the practice used. Whoever had written the program had decreed that whenever the word 'vegetarian' appeared by a patient's name a warning about 'inadequate diet' should be added to the records.

48

I received a letter today from an angry reader. She says that when she telephoned to talk to me on a radio programme she was told by the producer that I was a 'nutcase who will go off at a tangent if given the chance and as this is a live programme we can't risk him slandering a large conglomerate who may sue us.'

'What a sad statement regarding a so called professional man', she writes, wrongly assuming that I knew that callers were being told this. 'Have you not a grain of self respect? Do you not find it demeaning to be gagged by a third rate radio presenter on a third rate radio station?'

Why, I wonder, are so many people so keen to believe the worst?

49

'Your trouble is that you see things in black and white,' said a friend. He was right. I do see some things in black and white. Hunting and vivisection are black. I cannot see any white in these activities. There are those who believe that we should compromise in order to move forwards. I cannot see why we should compromise at all. We are right. They are wrong. End of argument.

50

Driving through the countryside I came across a hunt. What a barbaric, mean-spirited activity hunting is. If a gang of impoverished city dwellers drove around on motorcycles, intent on chasing and killing animals, they would undoubtedly all be arrested. A man in fancy dress on a horse was arrogantly holding up a whip to stop the traffic while a party of men and women in fancy dress clip-clopped leisurely by. I wound down my window and tried to open a debate on the cruelty of hunting. The man on the horse stared down at me with empty, unfeeling, unseeing eyes and then cracked his whip down hard on my car roof, doing a considerable amount of damage to the paintwork. I did not bother to complain to the police.

Driving around the countryside I often see the red-coated barbarians preparing for their evil rituals. They clutter up the roads with their horse boxes and pollute the countryside with their very presence.

For years I have successfully managed to avoid meeting any hunt followers. I keep out of dark corners and avoid the sort of slime covered holes where these creatures hide away.

But by accident I did once find myself in a room with a few of them. My first inclination was to leave the room as quickly as I could. But, as an ardent student of human nature, I thought it was probably time that I tried to understand what makes these stag and fox murdering creatures tick.

So, I metaphorically manacled myself to a chair and allowed a bunch of these miserable, perverted miscreants to speak.

The first, a chinless, dull, dark-haired fellow had the sort of incisive intelligence that one normally associates with house bricks. He probably spends his days working in council offices somewhere. Or he may be a hospital administrator.

His first argument was that stag hunting is essential. He claimed that stags are vermin and that some of them need to be killed. He said that if they weren't killed then they would cause untold damage to the farmland upon which they wander. I countered by pointing out, firstly that the hunt itself causes a considerable amount of damage to land and property and wildlife and, secondly, by arguing that if the stags do need culling (something I do not accept) then it would surely more reasonable and responsible to do so humanely.

The chinless, weedy hunt supporter got quite excited by this. A speckle of froth appeared upon his lips as his tiny brain struggled to send messages to his mouth.

'Ah,' he said, waving a podgy finger at me, 'but the stag enjoys the hunt.'

The second hunt supporter looked female. She was probably somewhere between 25 and 50 years of age and she wore a headscarf printed with pictures of men in red coats surrounded by hounds. She hesitated before speaking as though she found ordinary, everyday speech a difficult task. When she finally spoke she did so in a high pitched nasal whine that reminded me of a moped stuck in second gear.

'You don't understand the ways of the country,' she said, in a patronising tone. 'These creatures, foxes and stags and such like, have to be kept down. It's the way of the country. The hunt is a remarkably efficient and economical way to do it.'

I told her that I thought she'd probably make more sense if she stood up and communicated through another orifice.

The hunt supporter seemed baffled by this so I explained my thought in more detail. She reddened and then looked offended.

'My husband is very important,' she told me haughtily. 'Don't you dare speak to me like that.'

I gave her ten pence so that she could telephone her important husband and pass on my sentiments.

The third hunt supporter was male and dressed in a tweed jacket and a pair of old tweed trousers. He smoked small pieces of old under-felt in a battered pipe and his nose and cheeks were lined with purple veins. Any decent wine merchant would have probably given a tidy sum for the right to wring out his liver and sell the proceeds.

'You can't stop the hunt,' he told me. 'It's something that has been going on for centuries. It's part of life. It's an important social ritual. It's part of our heritage.'

I muttered something about smuggling, slavery and highwaymen, hanging, scurvy and press gangs.

'Well, it's perfectly legal,' said the man with the pipe. 'You can't stop hunting. And if you ever do the hunts will kill all their horses and dogs.'

And that really seemed to sum up the argument in favour of hunting.

After the two remaining hunt supporters had left I sat and thought about what I had learned. And I tried to understand what sort of person could possibly get any enjoyment out of hunting.

Here are the conclusions I came to.

The men are almost certainly inadequate and possibly sexually incompetent. The men who hunt or follow hunts are full of guilts and repressions. They carry around with them an enormous but unfulfilled sexual burden. They try to rid themselves of all their guilt by taking part in cruel and savage rituals. The women also have severe sexual problems. They are desperately repressed and deeply unhappy. They go hunting or follow hunts because they get little satisfaction from their sexual partners. They are desperate to be fulfilled but, like many evil folk, can only obtain release when blood is shed.

Those who hunt or follow the hunts are deeply unhappy people. They desperately need help.

Sadly, however, because they are unintelligent, invariably semi literate and inevitably cowardly they do not have the wisdom or the courage to ask for help. So we will do what we can to help them.

If you know anyone who goes hunting or who follows hunts you can help them in the following simple ways.

Try to make their lives as miserable as possible. Like most sadists these people also enjoy being maltreated. Inside every sadist there is a masochist trying to get out.

I know it sounds cruel but if you have a huntsman working for you then sack him. If you have a hunt supporter working on your payroll give him or her the push. They may seem aggrieved but in the fullness of time they will thank you for your kindness.

If a hunt supporter wants to join your club then blackball him. If a hunter wants you to mend his plumbing or service his car tell him to piss off.

Deep down these people know that they are foul and evil. They know that they need to be punished. They feel deep shame and guilt and by persecuting them you will be helping them.

51

Animal are the truly oppressed citizens of our world. Philosophers write long books about whether or not animals have rights. How can there possibly be any doubt? How can animals not have rights? Who gave us the right to decide whether or not animals have rights?

52

People seem to want easy solutions for everything these days. Everyone wants to get rich by winning the lottery. It is far easier to acquire a million pounds, dollars, marks or francs by winning a prize than it is by working.

No one who is fat wants to make any effort to lose weight. They want to take a magic pill and watch the fat drop off.

And no one wants to make any effort to avoid cancer or heart disease - they want doctors to find a cure for such diseases so that they don't need to worry and can carry on doing all the things which are known to be bad for them. The truth is that most cancers and most heart disease are avoidable. But most people don't want to be bothered. They don't want to give up their fatty foods. They want scientists to find a cure so that they can carry on as before.

It is this laziness, this eagerness to hand over the responsibility to someone else, this reluctance to accept responsibility for one's own destiny or to take action which might be troublesome, this unwillingness to deny oneself the harmful activities one enjoys, which sustains the morally- and intellectually-bankrupt cancer industry. And it is the wish to have someone else find an instant solution, a quick cure, which sustains the vivisectors. They are, they tell everyone, looking for a 'cure for cancer'.

'If I put a few coins in the collecting tin,' thinks the smoker or the over-eater, 'the scientists will find a cure and I won't have to give up the things I enjoy doing.'

And the smoker or the over-eater don't mind what the scientists do in their search for a magic cure.

They believe what they are told because they want to believe. And they are happy to accept the idea that animal experiments are done on their behalf (and with their few coins) because they believe that the animal experiments may enable the scientists to find that elusive but oh so convenient cure.

53

I had for years wanted to write a book listing examples showing that animals can be kind, thoughtful, sad, comforting - and, generally, exhibit the variety of emotions associated with human beings. The other day I found a note which I had written to myself seven or eight years ago which said simply: 'Book on animals' humanitarian behaviour: intelligent and kind behaviour; general and specific examples'.

When Elephants Weep: The Emotional Lives of Animals is written by Jeffrey Masson and Susan McCarthy and is just the book I would like to have written. (As an author I can think of no greater tribute to give). It is packed with examples showing that animals experience emotions. I found the book almost too moving to read. Here is one short extract from the book:

'In one grim and inexcusable experiment on fifteen rhesus monkeys, they were trained to pull either of two chains to get food. After a while a new aspect was introduced: if they pulled one of the chains a monkey in an adjacent compartment would receive a powerful electric shock. Two thirds of the monkeys preferred to pull the chain that gave them food without shocking the other monkey. Two other monkeys, after seeing shock administered, refused to pull either chain. Monkeys were less likely to shock other monkeys if they knew those monkeys, and were less likely to shock other monkeys if they had been shocked themselves.'

I am constantly ashamed to be a member of the same race as those who devise such experiments.

I am glad that Masson and McCarthy have already written this book. I really do find it distressing to be constantly reminded that animals have qualities which we, arrogantly, regard as uniquely human and I would have found it very painful to have to write such a book. This is, I suspect, why I never got round to writing the book.

54

Animals live to six times the age at which they reach maturity. If this was true for humans we would live to be well over 100. Since humans are the only animals to spend a fortune on health care, why are humans the only animals who don't normally live this long?

55

For years we've been told about the wonders of gene therapy. We've been told that by messing about with genes scientists will be able to eradicate disease and create wonderful new foods. But there has been far too little discussion about the dangers of gene therapy.

Now scientists, pundits and commentators all seem to have accepted gene therapy as a 'good thing'.

I am not so enthusiastic. I believe that messing about with genes is one of the greatest threats to mankind. If you have children then I think you should be worried: for the world you bequeath them may not be the world you know.

What worries me is not simply the prospect of a mad gene-manipulator producing a human baby with fins, a tail and horns (and don't believe anyone who tells you that that is impossible) but the fact that once you start messing around with genes you can, if things go wrong, change the whole nature of the human race.

What, for example, if someone makes a mistake and slips in a dominant gene that ensures that all white baby boys grow to be eight foot tall? Or what if somehow a gene that causes a rare disease gets mixed up with a gene that causes blue eyes?

What if politicians work hand in hand with genetic scientists and decide that some races should be 'altered' or even 'eradicated' in some way? What if a group of doctors, politicians and social scientists decide that in future everyone should be six feet tall exactly - and have blue eyes and blonde hair? (Those of you old enough to remember another Germany may have heard of something like that in the past).

What if the scientists decide that all women should have the same sized breasts? What if it is decided by decree that all children will look the same? What if the scientists impregnate a female monkey with human sperm in order to create a 'slave' being that can do routine daily tasks? (What would you say if I told you that I suspected that scientists have already done this?)

Genetic scientists say they will be able to tell you what diseases you'll get as you get older. But do you really want to know what horrors await you?

Food scientists will create animals and plants which will give us square eggs, bacon slices and tomatoes so that sandwich-making becomes easier. Do we need that?

I know the 'experts' will dismiss my fears as nonsensical. 'They' will, of course, insist that nothing can go wrong - and that there will be committees and regulations to make sure that nothing frightening happens. But accidents do happen. Experts said the Titanic was safe.

And one in six hospital beds are occupied by people who have been made ill by doctors. Since those medical errors weren't produced on purpose they must have been a result of medical accidents. Remember thalidomide? And the scores of other drug related health problems which have hit the headlines during the last few decades?

Time and time again scientists assure us that nothing can go wrong. And time and time again something does go wrong.

Remember Chernobyl?

To the risk of accidental disaster we must add the risk of fraud and corruption. Surprise, surprise, not all scientists are honourable and well meaning. Fraud and dishonesty in science are now common-place. A recently published book concluded that 12% of all research work in America is fraudulent.

With fraudulent and incompetent scientists playing around with our genes we could all be in big, big trouble - soon.

The idea of mad scientists using genetic experiments to create a master race, or interbreeding men and gorillas to create stronger work-ers used to be just science fiction. Now it is no longer science fiction. As writer Andrew Tyler put it in a paper in the European Medical Journal: 'The new gene technologies have the capacity to change eve-rything - to alter the actual physical fabric of every species on earth, our own included.'

Or consider leading economist, Robert Beckman. Writing in his book *Into the Upwave* he said: 'Theoretically, we can take the genetic structure of a rabbit's reproductive capacity and transfer it to a man, giving him the sexual reproductive capacity of the rabbit...'.

Genetic engineering now enables scientists to alter the genetic constitution of any animal or plant. But is that really what we want? Should we let scientists mess around with nature in this way at all?

Some scientists will claim that through genetic engineering they will be able to prevent some diseases appearing at all. They will be able to eradicate diseases which are transmitted through the genes. And that is undoubtedly an attractive proposition. But is the risk worth taking? Where do we make the scientists stop?

I think we should stop them now. I don't think the alleged com-mercial and economic advantages of genetic therapy to society are worth the risks.

56

'Of course we can splice genes. But can we not splice genes?'
Jean Paul Sartre

57

Animal researchers received a £100,000 grant to study how worms defaecate. Other researchers, who received £160,000, found that monkeys were less stressed by repeated electric shocks if they had a companion nearby. A third group of researchers, who received £71,000, found that male monkeys were more likely to get erections when there was a female monkey in heat nearby. Remember all this next time you are invited to put money into a tin for 'medical research'.

58

The truth is that animals can help doctors save human patients. But through observation - not experimentation.

Many vertebrates - including monkeys, pigs and elephants, use plants as medicines as well as food. Sick animals seek out and eat plants which they know will help them; they eat some plants, they hold others in their mouths (we call it buccal absorption) and they rub yet others onto their skin (we call that topical application). Ethiopian baboons who are at risk of developing schistosomiasis eat balanites fruits, which are rich in a potent anti-schistosome drug. Chimpanzees in Tanzania use a herb which has a powerful anti-fungal, anti-bacterial and anti-nematode activity. If they just ate the herb it wouldn't work because the valuable compound would be destroyed by stomach acidity. So they hold the leaf in their mouths in the same way that angina patients are encouraged to hold glyceryl trinitrate in their mouths to expedite absorption. Kodiak bears apply a drug topically which helps to kill parasites. They scratch the root into their fur. European starlings combat parasitisation to their nests by fumigating incubating eggs. Lethargic chimps with diarrhoea treat themselves with vernonia. Howler monkeys use herbal medicines to control birth spacing and to determine the sex of their offspring.

We can learn an enormous amount by watching other animals.

58

But instead of watching these sensitive, intelligent and thoughtful creatures the vandals in white coats cage them, torture them and kill them with all the scientific sense of youthful hooligans tearing the wings off flies.

In a generation or so our descendants will look back at the vivisectors and wonder not just at the sort of people they were, but at the sort of people we were to let them do what they did.

Animal experiments must stop. And they must stop now. For your sake; for your children's' sake; and for the sake of the animals the vivisectors kill.

59

'Like many of my contemporaries I had rarely for many years used animal food, or tea and coffee etc.; not so much because of any ill effects which I had traced to them, as because they were not agreeable to my imagination. The repugnance to animal food is not the effect of experience, but is an instinct. I believe that every man who has ever been earnest to preserve his higher or poetic faculties in the best condition has been particularly inclined to abstain from animal food.'

Henry David Thoreau

60

When a cat has died well meaning friends will sometimes say something like: 'Why don't you get another one?' This is rather like suggesting to bereaved parents that they just go out and adopt another child. Or, to someone whose parents have died, suggesting that they adopt a pair of old people they've never met before.

61

I read an interview with Henri Cartier Bresson in a newspaper. The legendary photographer described himself as a 'libertarian' and an 'ethical anarchist'. These are words with which I feel great sympathy. I am driven by the need to right injustice, fired by the exploitation of the weak, the dumb and the gentle and constantly saddened by the fact that the truth is no longer a treasured commodity.

62

People these days do not want wisdom, information or knowledge. They ask questions but do not want answers. They do not value experience. Everyone wants a quick, simple, slick solution. It is, I fear, the television age. We live in the age of thirty second sound bites; politicians and others produce meaningless three sentence homilies and people believe them. Those in the healing business offer quick solutions to problems which can only be solved by abstinence or self awareness.

The scientists who perform animal experiments rely heavily upon this yearning for quick solutions. They know that by promising 'magic bullet' solutions to diseases such as cancer they can excite the public into supporting their evil work. And to a large extent they are right.

The reality - that most cases of cancer and heart disease can be prevented - is of no importance. This is the media age and perception is far more important than reality.

63

There were three women, all wearing fur coats, looking into a shop window. Heaven alone knows how many animals had died so that these women could impress one another and make bold, traditional fashion statements to the world.

'These animal rights people who object to fur coats make me so angry,' said one of the women.

'I'm quite sure the animals are proud that their fur is used to make coats.' said another.

'My fur is made from animals which were especially bred,' said the third. 'If it wasn't for me those animals would have never lived at all.'

'If I didn't like animals why would I want to wear fur?' said the second.

I moved away.

But I felt guilt because those woman and I are members of the same species.

64

'The anti-vivisectionist has nothing to prove; many animals used in experiments are sentient and purposive and thus have prima facie rights to live and be left alone.'
Professor Arthur L Caplan

65

A hunt supporter accosted me one day. 'If you don't stop writing articles attacking hunting you'll get into trouble,' he said. 'Some very powerful people support hunting.' I said nothing.

'They'll stop you writing books,' he said. I said nothing.

'They'll set lawyers on you,' he said. I said nothing.

He thought hard, clearly frustrated. 'They'll put shit though your letterbox,' he said.

66

'One farmer said to me, 'You cannot live on vegetable food solely, for it furnishes nothing to make bones with' and so he religiously devotes a part of his day to supplying his system with the raw material of bones; walking all the while he talks behind his oxen, which, with vegetable made bones, jerk him and his lumbering plough along ·in spite of every obstacle.'
Henry David Thoreau

67

The world's vivisectors - the barbaric psychopaths who perform allegedly scientific experiments on animals - torture and kill countless millions of animals every year.

Every thirty seconds these Hitler-think-alike, pseudo-intellectual thugs get through around one thousand cats, dogs, puppies, guinea pigs, monkeys, baboons, chimpanzees, rabbits, hamsters, mice, rats and kittens.

They obviously need a constant supply of animals to satisfy their depraved needs. They often obtain monkeys, chimpanzees and similar animals from countries where these animals breed naturally. In some countries animals of this type are treated like vermin and can be hunted, captured and sold with no restrictions.

Mice needed for experiments are often specially bred.

But finding enough dogs and cats can be difficult.

In America where there isn't quite as much secrecy about these things it is now known that vivisectors regularly torture and kill former family pets.

Amazingly, around two million pets are stolen every year in the United States.

In one part of New York over 10,000 dogs were reported missing in a single nine month period. One bereaved pet owner searched for his missing dog and found him inside a research laboratory.

Animal theft is really big business there. Vivisectors prefer working with pet dogs and cats because they are tame and trusting - and less likely to bite or scratch.

I firmly believe that petnapping goes on in other countries too.

Tragically, I believe if your dog or cat goes out at night there is a real risk that he or she could be captured and sold to a laboratory. If a family pet has ever mysteriously disappeared it could have found its way into a vivisector's laboratory.

The vivisectors are truly evil and will stop at nothing to obtain the animals they need. They don't care about the law. They don't care about the fact that families may mourn the loss of their loved pet. All they care about is getting another fat grant and performing yet more useless and cruel experiments. Vivisection is a big, rich business which needs an endless supply of raw material.

And the raw material they need could be your much loved family pet. Scientists working in horror laboratories should have to prove the origins of every animal on their premises - to anyone who asks. Why should vivisectors be entitled to do their evil work in secret - behind locked gates? It is, after all, often public money which they are using to pay for these pointless and cruel experiments in torture.

Animal lovers who have lost pets should have the right to enter all laboratories at any time to search for missing animals.

68

Vivisectors are today's concentration camp guards. Remember: Mengele, the World War II concentration camp doctor, the Angel of Death feared by millions, was a vivisector.

69

You cannot be neutral about vivisection. If you aren't against it then you are for it. Anyone who doesn't fight in the anti-vivisection war is just as responsible for what is done as are the men and women in blood stained white coats who torture and murder in the name of science.

70

I watched a documentary film about Anne Frank and I cried as I watched how the Germans treated their concentration camp victims during the Second World War. I cried not just because of the way the Jews were treated by the vile barbarians of Nazi Germany but because the pain, the sorrow, the indignity and the cruelty suffered by Anne Frank and millions of others has changed nothing.

I believe there are plenty of people alive today who would happily operate concentration camps and gas chambers if the government told them to.

There are 20,000 vivisectors in this country. Evil men and women who will do anything for money. Evil beings for whom cruelty is a way of life and compassion just a meaningless ten letter word. The evil being who can ignore the pitiful screams of a kitten or a puppy can just as easily ignore the pitiful screams of a child.

71

I had a conversation with a newspaper editor. It went like this.

Editor: 'Why do you spend so much time writing about animals?'

VC: 'Because I like animals. I care about them. And I think they are treated badly.'

Editor: 'But you're wrecking your career. People think you're just a nutter.'

VC: 'I don't care. Isn't there anything you feel passionate about? Isn't there anything in your life which you think is worth fighting for?'

Editor (after thinking for some time, and clearly puzzled): 'What do you mean?'

72

There are, it cannot be denied, more things to worry about today than there have ever been before.

When we and our descendants look back on this period in our history there will be little for us to be proud of. Superficially the last few years have been a period of growth for a civilised, developed society. There are motorways everywhere. Most people own micro wave ovens, video recorders and television sets. The Channel Tunnel is open.

But the soul of our time has been sour and will leave a bitter taste. The second half of the twentieth century will be remembered with shame and embarrassment. Our time in history will be remembered as the decade when people stopped caring, stopped trusting one another and started thinking only of themselves. The second half of the twentieth century will be remembered for poverty and extravagance; for violence, hatred and jealousy.

The incidence of violence in our society is increasing faster than at any previous time. The incidence of child abuse is on the increase. Every winter thousands of old people die because they cannot afford to feed themselves or keep themselves warm. The number of people committing suicide is rising faster than ever. The number of people who have no jobs, and no hope of employment, has never been higher. The incidence of baby battering is on the increase. The number of people needing psychiatric help is increasing annually. A baby born today is more likely to be admitted to a mental hospital than win a place at university. Thousands of people are homeless and have no hope of finding homes. Millions of hard working people are technically bankrupt because they bought their own homes. There are now more alcoholics around than ever before - and the incidence is increasing every year. Politicians everywhere are a dishonest, untrustworthy bunch. We have polluted our environment, fouled our seas and filled our world with indestructible rubbish. We have more laws than ever before, and civil liberty is now merely a phrase from the past, but crime rises constantly. The greatest threat to personal liberty now comes not from crooks or bandits but from the courts and the police. Although we now have more social workers than ever before in our history, social problems are endemic in many areas of the world. We spend more on health care than ever before but people are sicker than ever and thousands of people die because they cannot get the treatment they need.

Most citizens have forgotten how to care and have become gutless zombies; more concerned about their chances of winning the Lottery than their responsibilities for the world.

Big companies that sell food, lend money or manufacture goods care nothing about their customers. They sell them food that will kill them. They lend them money they can't afford to borrow. And they sell them goods that are shoddy and poorly built. They lie and they cheat to maintain their profits.

The second half of the twentieth century will be best remembered for a meanness of spirit, a lack of generosity and an absence of honesty. But most of all our time will be remembered as the years when hardly anyone really cared.

Revolutionaries who dreamt of freedom, peace and compassion when they were twenty dream today of new triple tufted carpets, double glazing and ABS brakes. (Today's twenty year olds have missed out the dreams of freedom, peace and compassion and gone straight to the dreams of triple tufted carpets, double glazing and ABS brakes).

How many people have retained their teenage dreams? How many people can say that they are living the lives they dreamt of living when they were sixteen?

Nero was accused of fiddling while Rome burned. At least he did something creative. Today's free citizen spends around five hours a day watching television and no longer believes that he can make a

"Holes were drilled in the cat's skull. The cat had a series of fits. The experimenters prefer to use former pets since these are more docile and easier to manage."

"The two chimps were placed in a small metal container. After four weeks they became very depressed"

"In a lifetime a meat eater will consume 70 lambs, 10 cows, 20 pigs, 80 hens and 10 turkeys."

"The cat's front legs were broken in a vice. The wounds were deliberately infected. The cat took four weeks to die."

"Our succulent fresh lamb is served with new potatoes, green peas and home-grown carrots."

"The cat was fixed in an apparatus and a hole was made in its skull. A tube was placed in the hole and a series of chemicals poured down the tube, directly into the cat's brain. The cat remained conscious but was clearly irritated. It exhibited vocal signs of distress and struggled to escape."

"The dogs were covered with an inflammable liquid. The liquid was then ignited. All the dogs suffered severe burns and died within a few days."

"Researchers blinded two domestic tabby kittens by sewing up their conjunctiva and eyelids. The kittens were then placed in a special holder and horseradish peroxide was injected into their brains. The kittens were then killed."

difference.

I hate television. Over my shoulder I see the forces of darkness arraigned in suits of every shade of grey. And yet while these evil forces crowd daily closer the over-promoted talents of the television age dedicate their lives to endorsing violence and sucking people dry for cheap programming. The magic box is dominated by self-important, intellectually deprived presenters with expensive haircuts and cheap brains. Salacious and hypocritical but rarely courageous or original they have turned a potentially powerful medium into a tool of the state. The government is safe as long as the voters are more concerned with soap-land than with reality.

The electors sit slumped in front of their nightly five hours of watered down, two dimensional entertainment because they are too frightened to speak up; they are convinced that they cannot make a difference. They may occasionally still feel anger, frustration, alienation and bewilderment. But they dare not speak out for they fear for their own safety. They know that unemployment - and worse - beckons for those who stand up and speak.

(I remember I was once fired by a newspaper for the heinous crime of making readers think. The editor felt that this was not the sort of thing his readers wanted.)

Please do not let your life drift by. You really can make a difference. So dust off your principles, drag your dreams back out of the attic and scream and shout and let the evil ones know that you care and that you will not let them win. The abuse of animals is the greatest abuse of the twentieth century and the abuse of animals in laboratories is the greatest abuse of animals. It is done in the names of science, mankind, medicine, morality and the relief of suffering but it is an abomination, and an insult to our past our present and our future.

73

A medical editor invited me to write a short article explaining why I believed that animal experiments were of no value to doctors. The editor told me that they would also be publishing an article from a doctor who would argue that animal experiments were necessary. When the journal eventually published my article it chose to do so in what I thought was a rather unusual way. In addition to our two articles the

66

journal published page after page of letters from doctors around the world - doctors who had been given the chance to look at my article before it was published and write their comments about what I had written for inclusion in the same issue of the journal.

74

I received a letter the other day from a reader who wanted to know why I am so outspoken.

'I agree with much of what you say,' he wrote. 'But you would make far fewer enemies if you were more tactful. You make people feel uncomfortable.'

I am sure that reader is right.

I've been a newspaper and magazine columnist for thirty years and in that time I've been fired well over forty times. (I've also re-signed quite a few times too - having a tendency to resign if anyone so much as moves a comma in my copy).

I am old enough to know that I have two main problems.

The first is that I am honest. I say what I believe. And I don't care whether it is politically incorrect or gets me into trouble.

And my second big problem is that I care.

Neither of these are, I realise, fashionable virtues.

Indeed, I am sure that some people would regard honesty and passion as vices. We live in strange and rather awful times. Most people don't seems to give a stuff about anything any more. The world is full of people who don't care, won't take responsibility and are frightened to say what they think.

Unlike their predecessors modern politicians no longer resign.

And they get away with it because not enough people care.

Our streets are full of people who are homeless and impover-ished. No one cares. Our hospitals are decaying. Patients are treated without compassion or respect. The educational system is a sick joke. Illiteracy is commonplace. Huge swathes of our population are unem-ployable because they can neither write a letter nor add up a column of figures. Go into a shop to buy something and the chances are that you will be served by a surly, ignorant assistant who doesn't care a jot whether you buy something or not. If you do buy and it goes wrong they won't care about that either. We live in a world controlled by bureaucrats and faceless morons who neither think or care about what they do.

Have you tried telephoning a large company to complain? It's like talking to cotton wool. Bored complacency is endemic.

A friend of mine has just received a cheque from his insurance company. The accident which resulted in this modest payment occurred years ago. Over the months he has spoken and written to an endless series of grey faced bureaucrats. None of them seemed to care two hoots about the delay.

Another friend is waiting to go into hospital for an operation on her hip. She has been on the waiting list for over a year. No one gives a damn. When she rings up to try and find out what is going on the hospital staff are rude and offhand. They clearly regard all patients as a bloody nuisance.

We live in a world which is run by the incompetent and the uncaring, the unthinking and the unfeeling.

No one cares.

Well I refuse to apologise for the fact that I care.

I have nothing but contempt for people who sit on the fence and won't say what they think.

75

Make tomorrow a National Animals' Day

If you care at all about animals make sure that you make your voice heard.

Here are ten practical ways in which you can help the animals on your National Animals' Day.

1.   Be especially kind to every creature you meet. Stop and say a friendly "hello" to every cat, dog or other animal you see.
2.   If you aren't already a vegetarian or a vegan give up eating bits of dead animal this week. Remember that every steak, chop or other piece of meat you eat is part of someone's mother, father, daughter, son, brother or sister. You don't have to become a Christian, Catholic or Jew to stop eating meat. But you can't be a true, practising Christian, Catholic or Jew if you do eat bits of animal flesh. (The bible says: 'flesh with the life thereof, which is the blood thereof, shall ye not eat [Genesis 9.4]).

3.   Telephone the police next time you see an animal being treated cruelly. If the policeman you speak to refuses to take immediate action insist that he give you his name and number - and then complain to his senior officer.

4.   Write to the vice-chancellor of your local university. Ask if the university has any staff members who perform animal experiments. Tell him that unless he confirms that the university does not allow animal experimentation you will have nothing to do with his institution.

5.   Next time you visit a town or city take with you a bag of seed or crumbs and feed the birds.

6.   Write to your political representative and tell him that you will not vote for him or her again unless s/he confirms to you, in writng, that s/he is opposed to all forms of hunting.

7.   Make sure that any charities you support do not use any of their money for animal experiments.

8.   Write to your local television station, radio station and newspaper - and ask them what they are doing to help fight animal cruelty.

9.   If you buy eggs make sure that you only buy eggs which come from genuinely free range hens. Tell your local shop manager that you will not buy eggs from him again unless he can confirm that his products do not come from battery hens.

10.   If you see a programme or article supporting farming, animal experimentation or some other form of animal cruelty write to the advertisers which support that station or publication and tell them that you will boycott their products. And tell them why.

Finally - remember that your National Animals' Day need not come to a sudden end tomorrow night. Make every day of your life National Animals' Day and you will feel better for it.

PART TWO

QUESTIONS AND ANSWERS

'Never apologise for showing feeling, my friend. Remember that when you do, you apologise for truth.'
Benjamin Disraeli

Question
Why do you hate vivisectors so much?

Answer
Because they are all nasty little psychopaths who deserve to be buried up to their necks in the fast lane of the nearest motorway.

Question
I am 25 and I work in a large office. Even though I now live in a town I still ride regularly with a local hunt. Some of the people I work with don't understand why hunting is necessary to keep foxes and stags under control. Recently, they have started to make my life miserable. A few even refuse to speak to me. I have tried explaining to them that hunting is more than just a sport but they don't seem to understand. I would appreciate your advice.

Answer
Stop hunting. It is a barbaric and inhuman activity patronised and supported by lying, psychopathic lunatics. I am not surprised that your colleagues refuse to have anything to do with you. Why don't you take up bungee rope jumping instead? Try it with a 100 ft. rope and a 60 ft. jump.

Question

I have written to the authorities to complain about your column. You should not be allowed to get away with your campaign to stop animal experiments. I am sure that most readers probably feel the same way that I do. You are an anarchist and if I had my way there would be no room for you or people like you in this world. It is disgraceful that you put the interests of animals before the interests of people who have to earn a living in order to support their families. I work in a laboratory where we experiment on animals in order to do essential tests.

Answer

I receive between five and ten thousand letters and calls a week. About a dozen object to something I have written. I usually just toss them into the waste bin after reading the first two or three lines and forget about them. But yours was the most unpleasant letter I have received for weeks and after reading it I had to wash my hands in antiseptic in order to bathe away the thought that I had touched something that you had touched. I have spoken to one of God's personal assistants and been assured that the day you go to hell a couple of tons of petrol will be thrown on the flames. Your evil sins will ensure that you, like all other vivisectors, will fry for eternity. The sound of your sizzling fat legs will be drowned only by the sound of your screams of agony. But none of that diminishes the sorrow and sadness in my heart when I think of the innocent creatures who will suffer and die in your blood soaked hands in the days which precede your appointment with the golden flames of hell.

Question

I belong to a local group which is trying to stop a road being built through a beautiful stretch of countryside. The trouble is that there are several other local groups. In theory we all share the same aim but in practice we spend most of our time fighting one another.

Answer

People who care are, by definition, passionate. And because passion sometimes burns with blindingly bright light they often forget the fundamental driving force which inspired their fervour in the first place. Many pressure groups end up by doing more harm than good. They forget the fact that the house is on fire and spend their lives squabbling over which colour lavatory paper is most politically acceptable. I have little doubt that the anti-vivisection movement would have achieved its objective of stopping animal experiments decades ago if it hadn't been for thousands of petty jealousies, harmful infighting and overgrown egos. All you can do is to remind yourself each day why you are fighting and what you are fighting for. Try to stand aside from the petty arguments about what colour ink to use on the protest placards and just get on with the main battle.

Question

Your recent reply to a letter from a hunt supporter was quite outrageous. If you repeat your libellous comments about people who hunt we will take action against you.

Answer

In my view all hunters are cowardly, parentally challenged, intellectually deprived, sadistic, blood thirsty psychopaths and all hunt supporters are evil, odious little vandals with the presence and personality of snailshit. May your balls rot and drop off, may your TV set receive only Welsh channels and may your car never start. You are a pathetic, whingeing, snivelling, cryptorchid dickhead with the brains of a TV game show host and the wisdom of a highway bollard. How's that?

Question

I'm worried about the danger of my children catching Mad Cow Disease from cow's milk. Do you think milk is safe to drink?

Answer

To be honest I haven't the foggiest idea whether or not you or your children can catch Mad Cow Disease from drinking milk. And although the British government tells us milk is perfectly safe I wouldn't trust them to tell me the time. My view is that drinking milk is a gamble and if you like the idea of gambling with your children's health then let them keep drinking milk.

Question
Animal experimenters say that their work is vital. Don't you agree with them? If not why don't you ever appear on TV debating with vivisectors?

Answer
I have repeatedly stated that I believe that all vivisectors are evil. They claim that animal experiments are essential - and that without animal experiments human beings will die.

But I believe the scientific evidence clearly shows that animal experiments help no one. I don't think any patient has ever been saved by animal experiments. But I do believe that thousands have been killed because of animal experiments. I honestly believe that anyone who claims that animal experiments are essential or even useful is either an ignorant fool or a lying, scheming, bastard.

In my view vivisectors are as weak as they are ignorant, as gutless as they are pitiless.

I repeat the public challenge I have made scores of times before to all vivisectors.

Meet me in a full debate on live TV. (My only stipulation is that it must be live.)

Tragically, I fear that the vivisectors will not respond.

For I suspect that in addition to being evil vivisectors are all cowards too.

I wish I could smoke one or two of the mean spirited low life bastards out of the woodwork and into the bright lights of public debate. But I doubt if it will be possible. These toxic monsters won't debate with me - and won't defend what they do - because deep down in their shrivelled, malignant little hearts they know that they are wrong. And they know that they will lose.

I haven't debated with a vivisector for a long time. At the end of my last televised debate members of the studio audience were invited to vote by telephone. The question was simply whether or not all vivisection should be stopped. The two vivisectionists who wanted animal experiments to continue obtained 16% of the total vote. I (who argued alone) received 84% of the total vote.

Since then no vivisector has been willing to appear in the same studio as me.

Question
Did you receive any response to your challenge to vivisectors?

Answer
No. My challenge to vivisectors to meet me in a live TV debate has appeared in tens of millions of newspapers and magazines. Thousands of readers have sent copies of my challenge to universities, TV producers and individual vivisectionists. There cannot be a single vivisectionist anywhere who does not know of my challenge. But not one of them has the guts (or the courage of his convictions) to take me on in open debate.

And, remember, I am prepared to argue not only that animal experiments are entirely worthless and scientifically unsound but also that they have never been of any use at all to doctors. More than that - I believe that animal experiments are responsible for thousands of premature human deaths.

The vivisectionists will happily take on animal rights campaigners who are not medically qualified. But they all refuse to debate with me. Could it be because they know that if they dare to take me on in public debate the world will see the worthlessness of the evil practice of vivisection?

In the long gone days when vivisectionists would debate with me I never lost a single debate - always winning by a huge majority. I'm a useless public speaker but I won simply because the facts are on my side.

The medical and scientific evidence proves that I am right.

I believe that the thousands who perform and support animal experiments are fifth rate pseudo-intellectuals without the wit or wisdom of a pea between them. I believe they are cruel and self serving. I believe they are hypogonadal, anecephalic, emotionally stunted, spiritually deprived, amoral psychopaths.

What a pity they won't debate with me.

Question
I want to help stop animal experiments. What can I do?

Answer
Here are five things you can do to help stop animal experiments:

1. Write regularly to your political representative. Ask him what he is doing to stop animal experiments. Remind him that laboratory experiments endanger human lives - as well as needlessly destroying animals. Send him or her leaflets to read. Explain that no laboratory experiment has ever saved a human patient. And point out that vivisectors torture and kill 1,000 cats, kittens, puppies, dogs, chimpanzees, monkeys, rabbits etc. every 30 seconds.

2. Try to buy personal and household products which have not been tested on animals. Many anti-vivisection groups now produce lists of toiletries and chemicals which have not been tested on animals. Whenever you come across a product that you are not sure about write to the manufacturer and ask them whether or not they test on animals. Press for a direct answer. Try to buy products from shops and companies which never do any animal tests - and promise never to do any in the future. Never underestimate the power of your purse or wallet.

3. Send regular letters to newspapers, magazines and TV and radio stations. Ask producers and editors why they are not doing more to expose this twentieth century crime. Every time you see a pro-vivisection argument broadcast or published write and put the anti-vivisection arguments.

4. Join an anti-vivisection group and do everything you can to distribute their leaflets. The group I founded is called Plan 2000 and it produces many different leaflets. Help by distributing them to schools and colleges or to friends at work. Buy T shirts, mugs and badges to help raise money for the production of yet more leaflets and posters. The vivisectors are supported by big business - and have billions of dollars behind them. The anti-vivisection movement has to raise its funds in pennies. Despite that inequality we are winning!

5. Before you give money to any charity make sure that they don't spend money on animal experiments. Write and tell charities which perform animal experiments why you aren't going to support them. And if you find a charity which insists on continuing to pay for animal experiments organise protests to persuade other citizens not to contribute. Campaign and protest outside charity shops run by charities which give money to scientists who perform animal experiments.

Question
I am very lonely. I don't have any real friends and there is no one I can really trust.

Answer
Try talking - and listening - to animals. You should be able to obtain peace, comfort and good advice. Animals are honest, straightforward and, if unthreatened, generally full of love. These are not qualities which are widely available among members of the biped master species.

Question
How safe are genetically altered vegetables? My uncle says that gardeners have been genetically manipulating plants for centuries and that there is nothing to worry about.

Answer
Only a moron with an IQ smaller than his shoe size would eat genetically altered food. Today's scientists aren't just gently assisting nature to produce better and stronger plants. They want to create cubic potatoes (they slice up more neatly for chips) and mouth sized cauliflower for convenience. They'll use animal genes (including human genes) to do this. Buy a bagful of genetically altered fruit'n'veg and you'll have to lock your fridge at night to make sure that the carrots don't creep upstairs and eat you. If you're fool enough to eat a genetically altered tomato don't write to me in six months time to complain that you have suddenly turned bright red, become rather corpulent and got a funny green bit growing out of the top of your head. The goofy idiots in white coats say genetically altered food is safe. But that's what they said about thalidomide and Chernobyl.

Question
Why do you care so much about animals? Animals don't have feelings like us. My mate and I go out shooting cats in the evenings because there are so many of them that they're like vermin around where we live. Animal experiments are good because they keep animals under control. Humans are entitled to do what they like with animals

because humans are the most important species on earth. And if all the animals in the world had to be wiped out by experimenters so that I could live one day longer I'd think that was great. Animals are like coal and oil; they were put on this earth for us to use.

Answer
Like all those who support animal experiments you are clearly a being unencumbered by intellect, compassion or integrity. Your conceit and arrogance and your assumption that as a member of the human race you are inevitably superior to all other creatures reminds me of the abhorrent qualities exhibited by the Nazis. If I had to press a button to decide whether you or a mouse should live the mouse would get my vote. In a decade or so our descendants will look back upon those who now support animal experimentation with revulsion. Morally and ethically animal experimentation is repugnant. Scientifically and medically animal experimentation is indefensible. Please don't read my column any more. I don't like to think of you reading what I've written.

Question
Will you please ask your readers to help us stop the live exporting of calves and lambs?

Answer
I have long opposed the transportation of live animals and would urge all readers to urge their Members of Parliament to stand up in the House of Commons and publicly oppose this cruel and barbaric trade. Those who are involved in the transport of live animals do not have enough brainpower to respond to logic or good sense and so, until the law catches up with public opinion, their evil trade must be prevented by peaceful public protest. If you live anywhere near a port or airport where animals are shipped abroad then join in local protests to help stop this barbaric activity. But I want to go further than this. I would like to see people stop eating animals altogether. I like animals. They make good friends. And I may be odd but I don't like people eating my friends.

Question
At your suggestion I've attended quite a lot of protests about the exporting of calves. I've also protested about hunting. The police are invariably present at all these protests in quite large numbers. I always get the feeling that they are on the side of the people abusing animals.

Answer
The police seem to regard animal rights protestors as a major target. Since the vast majority of animal rights protestors are peaceful, sensitive, kindly folk who are no threat to the security of the nation some may feel that the police could be under orders from the politicians and are opposing those who campaign on behalf of animals because they are a threat to many large and powerful businesses. When £10,000 worth of damage was done to my motor car no policeman turned up to inspect the damage. I wonder if the police would have reacted in the same way if animal rights protestors had done £10,000 worth of damage to a lorry used to transport animals.

Question
Animal exports are legal and unless the law changes anyone who tries to stop them should be put in prison.

Answer
The gas chambers which the Germans used to get rid of millions of Jews were legal too. But there is a lot of difference between something that is 'legal' and something that is 'right'. There are times when the law is wrong and when protesting is right - and this is one of those times. Breeding and exporting animals is, quite simply, wrong and must be stopped. The sound a cow or ewe makes when her calf or lamb has been taken away from her is heartbreaking and I believe that the trade in animals is unforgivably barbaric. In my honest opinion saying that people will suffer financially if the trade in calves, sheep and other creatures is stopped is akin to arguing that closing down gas chambers was wrong because it was bad for the gas chamber manufacturers.

Question
I have an airgun and like shooting. I shoot birds but because I don't
want to risk hitting another person or breaking a window. I never aim
at birds when they are on the ground only when they are in trees. My
girlfriend has broken up with me. She says that what I am doing is
cruel but she has a cat that kills birds and she still loves the cat so why
doesn't she love me?

Answer
The fact that the cat is obeying a simple, primitive hunting instinct -
designed to keep it alive - whereas you are a sadistic, psychopathic
cretin getting your pleasure out of killing defenceless creatures purely
for fun may have something to do with it. Your girlfriend is obviously
sensible and sensitive whereas you are simply an insensitive and intellectually deprived thug suited only to a career in politics or the
pharmaceutical industry. I trust that your bank balance will always be
small, that you will be for ever besieged by worries, uncertainties
and guilt and that you marry an ambitious, pushy, razor tongued,
ball busting, shopaholic feminist with halitosis, herpes and a mous-
tache.

Question
I hate shopping at the local supermarkets because I invariably end up
surrounded by shoppers whose trolleys are full of bits of dead animal.

Answer
Speak to the manager of the store you use and ask him to introduce a
'vegetarian only' check-out. Supermarkets know that they have to
respond to their customers' demands if they are going to stay in business. If enough people request vegetarian check-outs then the shops
will introduce them.

Question
A friend of mine who is very conscious of environmental matters says
that he only eats 'green' meat. He seems to think that this means that
he is an animal lover. What is 'green' meat?

Answer

People who think that they ought to stop eating bits of dead animals, but whose primitive, physical yearnings for the taste of blood and flesh is stronger than their wafer thin consciences, often claim to eat 'green' meat. This does not mean that they eat rancid meat, retrieved from broken down freezers, but that they eat meat torn from the bodies of animals allegedly better looked after than most animals before being slaughtered. Since most animals are treated cruelly and barbarically by those who market their corpses simply giving 1,000 sheep a cheery wave at Christmas probably entitles the meat producer to describe the resultant meat as 'green'. The whole concept of 'green meat' is a marketing confidence trick of breathtaking audacity. Those who fall for the con and claim to eat 'green meat' are naive, insensitive, stupid and self deluding. People who eat meat are eating bits of dead body. No meat eater should ever be allowed to forget the source of the food on his plate.

Question

My boyfriend really annoys me. He is only ever concerned with himself. I am very concerned about a wide variety of political issues. I campaign about cruelty to animals and about environmental abuses. But he won't get interested in anything. He says it's all a waste of time. He says that 'they' won't ever take any notice of people like me so I'm wasting my time writing letters and going on marches. All he is interested in is his career, his car and having a good time. He works as a television presenter and when I try to get him to use his position to help my campaigns he refuses, saying it would damage his career to get too involved. I'm beginning to think that we might not be very well suited.

Answer

The world is divided into two groups of people: those who are selfish, narcissistic and self-obsessed and those whose concern for themselves is tempered or even overwhelmed by their genuine concern for some other aspect of life.

Individuals in the first group tend to become politicians or TV presenters and acquire far more power, money and fame than is good for them or anyone else. They find it difficult to understand why people like you get so upset about things that don't directly concern them.

People in the second group, like you, suffer endless agonies of guilt, frustration and anger because they know what is wrong with the world, they want to put it right and yet they find that those in power won't listen to their screams of outrage.

You, I'm afraid, are one of the unlucky ones. You are in the second group. You care. And you won't ever be able to escape from that burden.

Say goodbye to your shallow boyfriend. Your relationship has no future. He won't change and you can't. He will become increasingly irritated by your seemingly illogical commitment to change the world and you will find his conceit, self satisfaction, arrogance and aloofness increasingly insufferable.

Question

When we got married we had a vegetarian meal at the reception. Several relatives are now complaining that we should not have imposed our beliefs on other people. What do you think? We paid for the food and didn't want to spend our money paying for bits of dead animal.

Answer

Tell anyone narrow-minded enough to complain to piss off out of your lives. If you don't take a firm stance now you'll face more harassment if you ever make a contraceptive blunder and start a family. Moronic relatives will warn you that you must not 'impose your beliefs' on your unborn child. They would not, of course, expect you to bring your child up in the Jewish faith if you are Christian (or vice versa) so why the hell they should expect you to give the kid meat if you are vegetarian I cannot imagine. But they will.

Question

I am incensed at the way the government and the police are allowing - and even supporting - the export of live animals to the continent. What are your views?

Answer

Sheep, lambs, cows and calves and other 'farm' animals are treated like cars, cans of paint or bottles of jam.

But animals have feelings just like you do. Sheep and cows are sensitive, intelligent creatures.

Cramming anxious, nervous, live animals into lorries until they cannot move is barbaric beyond belief. Depriving them of food and water for hour after hour is vicious, inexcusable cruelty.

Question
My family has had two butchers shops for three generations. We have recently had to close, putting seven people out of work. We blame you and your articles about meat.

Answer
Thank you. I was feeling a little low until I opened your letter. I had just been told about a cow which had got its leg trapped. The farmer had sawn off the cow's leg (without an anaesthetic) so that he could sell the rest of the animal to the butchers. But your letter made me feel better. People who put meat on their shopping lists are writing themselves suicide notes. People who sell meat are in the double ended mass murder business: animals are killed to provide the meat and the meat then kills those who eat it. I hope that you will find something more useful to do with the rest of your life.

Question
I am a hospital nurse. You are wrong to condemn vivisection. Animal experiments are essential if scientists are to find cures for cancer, AIDS and other diseases.

Answer
According to a piece of unpublished, illiterate research done by the heavily sedated 97 year old Professor Josef Weissmantle of the Mengele Memorial Social Engineering Department at the downtown University of Barnstaple you are right. According to 3,847,184,027,185,290 highly qualified doctors and scientists you are a dangerous, out of date lunatic. I commonly favour a contrarian view on social and scientific matters (on the grounds that the majority is usually misinformed, prejudiced and incapable of coherent thought) but in this instance I'm happy to be going with the flow. I suggest that you ask your colleagues to give you a brain scan. I suspect that you may be a Friday

person - produced by God when he was looking forward to the weekend. The chances are that the scan will reveal that you have got your brain in upside down and need urgent remedial surgery. Meanwhile, I have arranged for the hospital where you work to keep you on permanent bed pan duty on the diarrhoea ward.

Question
What do you think of the five year rule used by some companies which claim not to test their products on animals.

Answer
I'm not at all impressed by it. The five year rule means that a company can't sell a product that has been tested on animals, or which contains ingredients which have been tested on animals, until five years later. This means that companies which follow the five year rule, will be able to sell animal blood stained products as long as the blood stains are five years old. Ingredients tested in 1992 can be used in 1997 and ingredients tested in 1997 can be sold in the year 2002.

Personally, I think the five year rule is pretty useless. How can animal tests on cosmetics ever be stopped as long as the five year rule exists? I do not buy cosmetics from shops or companies which operate a five year rule.

Question
The family who live next door to me are all Christians. They go to church several times a week and always have posters containing sayings from the bible in their front window. They do not like animals and the week before last I saw them throw a bucket of water over one of my cats just because he was sleeping in their garden. He was weak and old and could not move very fast. He contracted an infection and yesterday I had to have him put down by the vet. When I confronted my neighbours they told me that God doesn't mind what people do to animals because they have no souls. Is this true?

Answer
Animals have souls. So-called Christians who claim otherwise will fry. When I mentioned the fact that some allegedly religious people say that it's OK to eat animals or use them in experiments because

only humans have souls two of God's assistants had to hold Him down. He was so furious that He wanted to flood America, send a plague of insurance salesman knocking on doors across Europe and press a button that would have ignited every volcano south of Aberdeen. Every thunderbolt He sends to earth has carved upon it the words: 'Animals have souls'. But only true believers can see the message. The children of the Devil see only a big flash and hear a lot of noise.

Question

I was interested to read about tamoxifen in your book *Power Over Cancer*. I was asked to take part in the experiment you described but I refused because I had heard that tamoxifen could cause cancer of the liver. I did not realise that it also could cause cancer of the uterus.

Answer

The experiments which showed that tamoxifen caused cancer of the liver were conducted on animals. Experiments also showed that tamoxifen causes gonadal tumours in mice. This evidence was, quite rightly ignored by the organisers of the trial and the government - presumably because they recognised that animals are so different to people that animal experiments cannot be replied upon. This is not unusual. In my book *Betrayal of Trust* I named dozens of drugs which cause cancer and other serious diseases in animals but which the government has licensed to be prescribed for human patients.

Question

I work in an abattoir. I object very strongly to your attacks on meat. Experts say that meat is an essential part of a healthy diet.

Answer

Which experts are you referring to? Traffic wardens? Accountants? Butchers? Meat is no more an essential part of a healthy diet than is coal, blancmange or stewed concrete.

Incidentally, have you seen the paper published by the Journal of Occupational Medicine and entitled *Cancer Mortality Among White Males in the Meat Industry*? The authors studied 13,844 members of a meat cutter's union and reported that a 'statistically significant proportional mortality ratio of 2.9 was obtained for Hodgkin's disease among abattoir workers' and that: 'The results suggest that the excess risk of death from Hodgkin's disease in abattoir workers may be associated with the slaughtering activity'. They also found that meat packing plant workers were more likely to develop bone cancer, cancer of the buccal cavity and pharynx and lung cancer than workers in other industries. The authors of this paper also named viruses which naturally cause cancer in cattle and chickens and pointed out that these viruses are present not only in diseased but also in healthy cattle and chickens destined for human consumption. 'Evidence suggests that consumers of meat and unpasteurized milk may be exposed to these viruses. It would appear, therefore, that these viruses present a potentially serious public health problem.' Other researchers have made similar discoveries about a link between the meat industry and the development of cancer. A study of 300,000 adult white males in Washington State in the United States of America showed a 'statistically significant elevated risk of death from cancer of the buccal cavity and pharynx among butchers and meatcutters'. If bits of dead animal give cancer to the people who handle them what the hell do you think they do to people who are daft enough to actually eat the stuff?

Question
My colleagues and I have complained to the publisher of your newspaper, the Press Complaints Commission, the General Medical Council, and the British Medical Association about your outrageous attacks on vivisectors.

Answer
Piss off. I don't give a stuff about you but I care passionately about animals. I believe that all vivisectionists are intellectually retarded, emotionally empty, spiritually dead psychopathic dickheads with the combined brains of a pustule. Now you can complain again, can't you? Maybe you should add the Royal Automobile Club and the Automobile Association to your list.

Question
I like animals but a friend of mine insists that animal experiments are essential and that those who oppose animal experimentation are dangerous lunatics.

Answer

Your friend is wrong; it is the vivisectionists who are dangerous lunatics.

My campaigns on behalf of patients have made me many enemies. During the last two decades I have been threatened in many ways. But my attempt to stop pointless, cruel and barbaric experiments on animals has made me more enemies than any of my other campaigns.

I have received a number of death threats from supporters of vivisection. Those threats were clearly intended to be intimidating and to stop me campaigning to stop this evil practice. The lives of the animals who live with me have been threatened too.

These very real physical threats show several things.

First, they show that my campaign to stop animal experiments is taken seriously by the mindless, cruel barbarians who perform and support animal experiments.

Animal experiments are valuable because they enable huge international drug companies to put new drugs on the market without testing them adequately on human tissues and human volunteers.

Why are animal experiments so valuable? Simple. If tests show that a drug doesn't damage a particular animal the company making the drug gets a licence on the grounds that the drug is safe. If tests show that a drug makes an animal ill the company making the drug still gets a licence on the grounds that animal experiments cannot be relied upon. I know it sounds crazy but that is just what happens. Your life and the lives of your children are endangered by this profitable policy.

When we succeed in stopping animal experiments drug company profits will collapse because drugs will have to be tested properly.

None of those who support animal experiments will debate with me on scientific or medical grounds on TV or radio. They know that they cannot win the intellectual argument.

My researches have produced evidence enabling me to prove that animal tests are useless and misleading. (The research is detailed in my book *Betrayal of Trust*, published by the European Medical Journal and available through all libraries).

Please help me stop animal experiments. And if I suddenly disappear please don't give up the fight. The forces of evil are powerful. But we will win. We will win because we are morally right, ethically right, scientifically right and medically right.

Question
You haven't written about hunting recently. Does this mean that you have given up your attempt to get it banned?

Answer
I regard hunting as an obscene activity, practised and enjoyed by the dregs of the middle classes who think that they are achieving gentility by clambering up onto horses, joining the hideous armies of the apocalypse and galloping around killing animals. Unreliable research has shown that male hunters are invariably decerebrate and impotent while all women who hunt are boring old sex-starved slags who climb on horses purely for the clitoral stimulation.

Question
I want a new year's resolution. Can you recommend something that will improve my health. I don't smoke and I exercise regularly.

Answer
Give up eating meat. There is nothing you can do that will improve your health more effectively than giving up meat. Numerous researchers have linked protein with cancers of the breast, prostate, endometrium (lining of the uterus), colon and rectum, pancreas and kidney. And the type of protein which is most likely to cause cancer is protein obtained from meat. The United States Surgeon General's Report 'Nutrition and Health' said: 'In one international correlational study... a positive association was observed between total protein and animal protein and breast, colon, prostate, renal and endometrial cancers'. The Surgeon General also reported that: 'Studies have also found an association between breast cancer and meat intake (Lubin et al 1981) and an association of meat, especially beef, with large bowel cancer among Japanese (Haenszel et al 1973)...'. One possible reason for the meat-cancer link may be the fact that chemicals such as DDT tend to accumulate in animal tissues - and may be found in animal tissues years after their usage has been controlled or stopped. Whether it is the chemicals in animal protein which cause cancer is, however, a question of rather theoretical interest: the important point is that meat causes

cancer. Japanese women who eat meat daily have more than eight times the risk of breast cancer compared to women who rarely consume meat. There have also been several reports showing a high correlation between meat and colon cancer. Beef has been specifically named as one type of meat associated with colon cancer. Several studies have shown a relationship between the incidence of prostate cancer and the consumption of animal protein. Because most people who eat a lot of meat usually also eat a great deal of fat (because meat often contains a lot of fat) it is difficult to know whether these links between meat and cancer are a result of the protein in the meat or the fat in the meat. It is also possible that the link between meat and cancer is a result of mutagens being formed during the cooking of meat. And some experts have pointed out that carcinogenic fat soluble contaminants such as drugs and pesticides may explain why meat causes cancer. However, I regard the question of how meat causes cancer as being of largely theoretical interest. The fact is that meat can cause cancer so if you care about your health you should stop eating it.

Question
I am 16. I do not like the idea of eating dead animals but I want to be a body builder and I have been told that without eating meat I will not get big. Indeed, I have been warned that it is not safe for me to train in the gym if I eat a vegetarian diet. Is this true?

Answer
No. It is not true. It is bullshit. Talking of bulls, bulls don't eat meat. Elephants don't eat meat. Baboons don't eat meat. They all get much bigger than you'll ever want to be. Many successful triathlon winners and body-builders are vegetarians. I am 6 foot 3 inches tall, weigh around 14 stone and can hold a pencil unaided. I don't eat meat.

Question
My two teenage daughters say that eating meat is cruel. They have both become vegetarians. They say that when animals are taken into an abattoir they must be frightened and that this means that the levels of adrenalin in their blood must increase. They've read somewhere that this increase in adrenalin levels could lead to illnesses such as high blood pressure and heart disease. Do you think that eating meat

taken from dead animals could be dangerous? If not how do I persuade my daughters to start eating meat again. I am worried that they will become ill if they stick to a vegetarian diet.

Answer
It isn't just the amount of adrenalin in dead animals which worries me (though I have said that this could cause problems). But what if a cow had a small cancer developing? I know animals are inspected but the inspections can't possibly be close enough to pick up small, developing cancers. This means that next time you sit down to tuck into a steak you might end up chewing a lump of cancer. Can you get cancer by eating it? I don't know. Nor, I suspect, does anyone else. There is no reason why your daughters should suffer ill health if they stick to a vegetarian diet. On the other hand, I believe that you are exposing yourself to a wide range of disorders by eating bits of dead animals.

Question
Since I read your recent comments about vivisection I have not been able to sleep.

Answer
Good. That was the idea. Man's abuse of and cruelty to animals is the most wicked crime of modern times. And vivisection is the most evil abuse of animals. If you want to know how to help fight vivisection contact Plan 2000 - the group I founded (but no longer run because it has grown too big!).

Question
I strongly object to your articles attacking scientists who perform animal experiments. Animals were put on earth by God so that man could use them.

Answer
I can sum up everything I wish to say to you in just two words. The second word is 'off'. I doubt if you are intelligent enough to guess the other word without any help so here is a clue: it is a four letter word which rhymes with 'luck' and starts with the sixth letter in the alpha-

bet. You should get the answer by teatime on Wednesday.

Question
My doctor and family want me to go into sheltered accommodation. I am 72 years old and quite fit but they're worried that if something happens to me I won't be able to call for help. However, the place they have recommended won't allow me to take Henry, my cat, with me. Henry and I have been together for nine years and I can't bear the thought of us being parted. My doctor even suggested that I should have Henry put down if I couldn't find someone else to look after him.

Answer
I suggest that you stand your ground and refuse to move until your doctor or your relatives have found a place where you and Henry can live together. You'll probably need to rely on your relatives since your doctor sounds as though he has the brains of a hubcap and as much talent for empathising as mud.

Despite the existence of an enormous amount of evidence showing that pets are just as important to health as human relationships some so called health care professionals still seem to treat cats, dogs and other animals as of no more consequence than cheap furniture. The result of this ignorance can be devastating. Old people who have been made to abandon their pets often become severely depressed and may die of guilt, anguish and a broken heart.

It is not uncommon for elderly or disabled individuals to refuse to move when they are told that they can't take their pets with them. And many old people refuse to go into hospital at all because they fear that while they are away their pets will be removed.

Not all nursing homes and sheltered accommodation cater for pets and that's fine because not all old people want to live surrounded by animals.

But there are places which cater for old people who want to keep their pets with them. And I strongly recommend that you insist on being found space in such a centre.

Question
A lot of people near where I live have animals but don't look after them properly. I know one house where 20 rabbits are kept in two

small cages. And I know people who have dogs but never take them for walks or look after them. People who acquire animals as pets should realise that there is a lot of responsibility involved.

Answer
Looking after animals properly takes time and money - and is a long term commitment. If you know someone who doesn't look after an animal properly you have a moral responsibility to report them to the police - once you've done this make sure that the police take action to stop the cruelty. (If they hesitate point out that mistreating an animal is behaviour likely to cause a breach of the peace).

Question
Is it true that capsules are made of gelatin - an animal compound? I am a vegetarian and worried by this.

Answer
Yes. Most capsules are currently made from gelatin. But it is perfectly possible to make capsules from vegetable cellulose. Drug companies will only do this when they get enough letters from patients protesting about their continued use of gelatin capsules. It is up to you to help change things.

Question
My husband and I have just got back from a holiday in Spain. It was a nightmare. There were cats all over the place - all hungry and thirsty, some dying. We went out morning and night taking food and water to them but couldn't carry enough food to feed them all. It broke my heart and I cried every day. I will never go back to Spain ever again. What can I do to help these poor creatures? I feel so helpless.

Answer
One can change some things with logical arguments and reasoned debates. Other things have to be changed by the judicious application of suffering. Naughty children sometimes only learn by being deprived of regular doses of television and I suspect that the Spanish will only start treating animals kindly when forced to do so through economic

sanctions. Write to the Ambassador at the Spanish Embassy and tell him that you will never go back to his blood soaked country until his fellow countrymen start treating animals with respect. Spaniards are primitive, rather simple minded people who have few natural skills and rely entirely on their climate to make a living. But they have some native cunning and will start treating animals decently if they understand that the alternative is a boycott by holidaymakers. Economic boycotts helped win freedom for blacks in South Africa and will help win freedom for animals around the world.

Question
I am fed up with your drivel about animals. I am a diabetic and without experiments on animals I would be dead.

Answer
I am afraid you have been conned (probably not a difficult task) by the evil money grubbing vivisectionists who want animal experiments to continue. Diabetics with brains campaign strongly for the abolition of vivisection. The first link between the pancreas gland and diabetes was established in 1788 without any animal experiments. And it was 22 years before that - in 1766 - that another doctor showed that the urine of diabetics was loaded with sugar (again, without animal experiments). Throughout the 19th century scientists wasted time performing useless animal experiments. If vivisection had been banned two centuries ago diabetics would have benefited enormously. History shows that progress in medicine is usually made by observant clinicians and never by white coated sadists torturing animals in laboratories.

  The vivisectionists are responsible for almost as much human misery and almost as many human deaths as animal misery and animal deaths. Incidentally, are you sure that your diabetes is controlled properly? Your letter rather suggests that you might be suffering from brain damage.

Question
How do vivisectors sleep at night? I don't think I could live with myself if I spent my days torturing animals for a living.

Answer

I am convinced that all vivisectors - and vivisectionists - are complete psychopaths. They do not have any of the normal feelings or emotions exhibited by healthy, individuals. Indeed, I believe that many of them obtain great pleasure from plunging a knife into a tethered, live animal and watching it squeal and scream in agony. These are people who are so oily, so low down, that they do not have to open doors to go through them - they simply ooze underneath them. Can you imagine the conversation when a vivisector gets home. 'Did you have a good day, dear?' 'Wonderful! I tortured another 43 cats - and some of them are still alive so they'll suffer all night and then I can have another go at them tomorrow.' Here is my list of ten individuals who would have made great vivisectors if they had not been busy doing something else:

1. Jack the Ripper
2. Attila the Hun
3. Dr Crippen
4. Heinrich Himmler
5. Satan
6. Adolf Hitler
7. Tomas de Torquemada
8. Cesare Borgia
9. Joseph Stalin
10. Benito Mussolini

Question

We wrote to our local university to ask them to debate with you about vivisection. They refused, saying that the last time anyone from the university spoke up in support of animal experiments a window was broken.

Answer

Gosh. A whole window? Did lots of policemen rush around to look at the damage? I've lost count of the number of windows I've had smashed. When £10,000 worth of damage was done to my car the police didn't even come and look at what had been done. As far as I am aware no one was arrested. Since I started my campaigns on behalf of animals and people papers have been stolen, I have repeatedly been threatened, my phone has been tapped and private detectives have been hired to investigate me. I now live behind locked gates to protect my animals. I know a lot of readers wrote to their local universities challenging vivisectors to debate with me. Not one had the guts to take me on.

Question

As a regular reader of your column I gave up meat last year. I now feel ashamed of myself for ever eating meat. I can't understand how I ever managed to eat bits and pieces of dead animals. But even more I cannot understand how seemingly normal men and women can murder and then sell bits of animals. I used to have several friends who were farmers but I no longer see them.

Answer

Meat and tobacco and the twin killers of our age. Anyone who sells or deals in these products is, quite simply, a mass murderer. But the seller of meat is a mass murderer twice: he is responsible for killing the beings he sells. And he is responsible for killing the beings to whom he sells those corpses. I confess that I do not understand how those who are involved in this, brutal, evil activity can sleep at night. These are people who are strangers to their own consciences. Within a decade, as the full horrors of Mad Cow Disease become apparent and as more doctors accept that I am right and that meat does cause cancer, the government will have to start stamping health warnings on hamburgers, sausages and steaks. By then it will be far, far too late. Hundreds of thousands of people - possibly millions - will have died simply so that farmers, slaughterhouse men, butchers and others involved in this bloody, unwholesome and unforgivably wicked trade can continue to make pots of money.

Question

I have a close relative who is chronically ill. I object strongly to your campaign against animal experiments. In fact I think you are disgusting and should be taken out and shot. People like you are like vermin. I would exterminate you all like the Germans tried to do to the Jews. If scientists are not allowed to continue to experiment on animals they will never find a cure for the disease which affects my relative. It is a pity that you don't like human beings as much as you like animals.

Answer
I fear that you have been misled by those malevolent, oleaginous legions who, for their own crude and personal commercial reasons, want animal experiments to continue. The truth is that animal experiments have never been of any help to doctors - and never will be. Indeed, animal experiments are so misleading that they endanger human life and are responsible for almost as much pain and suffering among human beings as among animals. My passionate campaign to stop animal experiments is driven by my love for people as well as animals. If you genuinely care about your relative you will join my campaign to halt the waste of time, money on resources on the hideous and barbaric practice of animal experimentation. When ordinary people see animals they tend to find them rather attractive and likeable. When vivisectors see animals they drool at the mouth and think: 'I'd like to torture that animal. I'd like to inject it with toxic chemicals and then kill it.'

Question
I do not approve of animals being used in horrific scientific experiments. I have told my doctor that I will not take any medicine which has been tested on animals. Do you have a list of drugs which I can take?

Answer
I believe that murdering, cowardly vivisectors (who have a collective IQ lower than the average winter temperature in Iceland) torture and kill around 1,000 cats, kittens, puppies, monkeys, dogs, rabbits and other animals every thirty seconds and that some of those animals are pets which have been stolen; I also believe that animal experiments are of absolutely no scientific value and are performed for purely commercial and personal reasons. There is, therefore, clearly no need for you to avoid essential drug therapy.

Question
It is not true that laboratory animals are kept in poor conditions. Ani-

mals in laboratories are extremely well looked after.

Answer

Every 30 seconds evil laboratory scientists kill another 1,000 animals. A huge international industry keeps wicked, heartless vivisectors supplied with a wide variety of animals. Some of the animals in the vivisectors' cages are specially bred. Some are captured in the wild and transported around the world. Others are family pets which have been captured and then sold into slavery.

Vivisectors claim that the animals they torture and kill are well looked after before and during experiments. This is a lie.

Animals are often kept in tiny cages for years - alone, terrified and able to hear the screams and cries of those creatures ahead of them on the death list. I've unearthed the official figures for the amount of floor space animals are allowed in laboratories - and the length of time they could spend in those cages.

You might like to measure out the size of these cages on your living room carpet. And then imagine the horror of your family pet living in a cage like that for years - without love or companionship, in constant fear and probably in severe pain too.

1. Dog
Possible life expectancy: 35 years
Size of cage: 8 square feet

2. Cat
Possible life expectancy: 20 years
Size of cage: 3 square feet

3. Rabbit
Possible life expectancy: 15 years
Size of cage: 3 square feet

4. Monkey
Possible life expectancy: 30 years
Size of cage: 6 square feet

5. Rat
Possible life expectancy: 4 years
Size of cage: 0.4 square feet

6. Mouse
Possible life expectancy: 3 years
Size of cage: 0.4 square feet

7. Guinea pig
Possible life expectancy: 7 years
Size of cage: 0.7 square feet

8. Hamster
Possible life expectancy: 2 years
Size of cage: 0.34 square feet

Question
I am worried that the company I work for may be supplying equipment to a laboratory where experiments are performed on animals. Would you please find out for me whether or not my fears are justified? If they are then I will do my best to get my company to stop. I am opposed to animal experiments.

Answer
I am afraid that my day, like yours, has just 24 hours in it. I have applied for an exemption from this unfair restriction but unless my application is treated favourably by the authorities I simply cannot check out every company in the world to find out which ones are supporting animal experiments. However, you can check the company out yourself quite easily - and I believe it is your responsibility and duty to do so. If the company you work for is supplying vivisectors and will not stop I sincerely hope you will resign immediately. In my opinion people who knowingly supply and support vivisectors are just as responsible for the horrible and pointless things done in the laboratories as are the vivisectors themselves.

Question
I don't know why you make so much fuss about people eating animals. I love a bit of fresh lamb.

Answer
The word 'fresh' attached to 'lamb' means that just a few days before you started to eat its corpse the lamb was running around in a field,

"This Maltese kitten is looking to see if it is safe to come out of its hiding place. If local children spot it they will use it as a football or throw it into the sea."

"Two days after the lamb was injected with the drug being tested it had a series of fits and vomited. It died shortly afterwards."

"The cat was shot in the head. It died 90 minutes later."

"The sheep were crammed so tightly into the lorry that none of them could move. One of them had a leg sticking out of the side of the lorry and must have been in great pain. The journey lasted 36 hours."

"The chemical was dropped directly into the rabbit's eye. After 24 hours the eye had become red and clearly irritated. Within 48 hours the eye was opaque and suppurating and the animal was clearly in pain. After 72 hours the rabbit was blind."

"The cat was force-fed with a household detergent until it died"

"The cat was kept in a small cage and given daily injections of the drug being tested. After three months the cat had lost all its hair and had developed a serious skin condition. It became blind and lost control of its bowels. The cat was kept alive for three years and then the experiment was terminated,"

Vernon Coleman and a sheep (Vernon Coleman is on the right)

playing with other lambs. The lamb's mother will not understand why her baby has disappeared and will probably still be searching desperately for it. Ewes love their lambs just as much as mothers love their babies. If this does not put you off eating 'fresh lamb' then you have deep-rooted psychopathic tendencies and I am glad that you are there and I am here.

Question

You are stupid not to eat meat. Farm animals are not like pets. Cows, pigs and sheep are bred to be eaten.

Answer

You are quite wrong and may well be already suffering from Jacob-Creutzfeldt disease - the human equivalent of Mad Cow Disease. Do not make any long-term holiday plans. Cows, pigs and sheep are just as affectionate, caring, loving and sensitive as cats and dogs. It is only our culture which has decreed that dogs and cats get well looked after while cows, pig and sheep get eaten. In other parts of the world the rules are very different. There is, for example, an old Korean saying that goes: 'A dog is not for Christmas - it will last well into the New Year'. Nice, eh?

Question

I hunt regularly. I object very strongly to your recent diatribe against hunting. If you repeat your attacks on hunting I intend to take legal action against you. You will find that this time you have bitten off more than you can chew.

Answer

I realise that people who hunt, like vivisectors and butchers, are not bright. Most, indeed, are so thick that they have to go to special evening classes to learn how to shout 'Tally ho!'. Here are two little word puzzles to keep you busy all week. First, the letters F.O. sometimes, but not always, stand for Foreign Office. What else do you think they might stand for? Second, I feel that people who hunt are best described with a word which rhymes with hunt but begins with another letter of the alphabet. The third letter of the alphabet. So, what is the word? Once you've worked out the answers write them on a postcard, together with your name and address, and send them to anyone you know who supports hunting.

Question
If you are right and vivisection is useless can you explain why scientists do experiments which are of no possible value?

Answer
The answer can be summarised in one word: money.

Animal experiments are cheap, fast and easy to perform. Vivisectors do not have to worry about satisfying ethical committees. They do not have to be very bright to perform an experiment on animals. They do not have to wait a long time for the results. And drug companies love animal experiments and will pay vast quantities of money for them because they know that if an experiment shows that a drug causes cancer or some other serious problem the results can be dismissed as irrelevant - on the grounds that animals are different to people - whereas if a drug does not produce any obvious signs of disease when given to an animal the results can be used to launch the drug for human use. The wonder is not so many animal experiments are performed but that the evil psychopaths do not do even more.

Question
I support your views on animals but I dare not make my views known in public. My mates would think I was soft.

Answer
I sometimes wear two small, silver ear rings in the shape of tiny rabbits. They were very cheap (less than £2 for the pair) but I rather like them. I was sitting on a train when it stopped at a platform. Two punk girls walked by the train window. One of them noticed one of my ear rings. She stopped to stare. She shouted to her friend and pointed at my ear ring. The friend stared. They giggled and laughed and put their tongues out at me. Then they called to a boy who was standing a few yards down the platform. He, like them, was dressed entirely in heavily studded black leather. He, like them, had huge silver ear rings hanging from both ear lobes. His nose, like theirs, was pierced. All three of them had tattoos on their hands and cheeks. The boy looked at

my tiny ear ring and glowered at me. He made a rude gesture with his hands and sneered. All three shouted something I couldn't hear. (I doubt if I would have been able to understand what they were saying even if I had heard them since the whole incident took place in a country where the populace speak a language of which I do not know one word). And then my train slowly pulled out of the station, leaving the three punks standing on the platform gesticulating, shouting and sneering at my tiny ear ring. (They could only see one).

I wondered why the three punks had objected. They were presumably dressed the way they were because they wanted to make a statement that they were different to the rest of society (even though they were dressed identically to one another and were, therefore, fashion slaves just as much as the company employee who wears a dark suit, a white shirt and a sombre tie). So I found it difficult to believe that they objected to my rabbit ear rings solely because they were 'different'.

The only other conclusion I could reach was that they objected because they regarded the rabbit ear rings as strangely 'soft', 'effeminate' and unsuitable for a man to wear.

Caring for and about animals is regarded as rather effeminate. It is not something which a 'real man' does. A real man drinks beer, eats lots of steak, smokes untipped cigarettes and has a heart attack in his forties.

Question
How can I find out whether or not the pills my doctor gives me have been tested on animals. I will not take anything - even if it means putting my life at risk - if it has involved the suffering or death of an animal.

Answer
I do not know of any drugs which are not tested on animals. But the tests that are done are pointless, entirely irrelevant and thus without consequence. There is no need to avoid drugs because of animal tests. Just keep fighting to stop all animal experiments.

Question
Your outrageous attacks on vivisection are totally unjustified. The animals which are used in experiments are always well looked after.

Answer
Lecturing abroad a little while ago I met a man who told me that his company did a lot of testing on rabbits.

The scientists shaved the rabbits so that they could 'paint' chemicals onto bare skin to see what happened.

To speed things up they started dipping the live and conscious rabbits into acid to burn off their fur.

The man I met told me that he and his colleagues complained that the noise of the screaming rabbits made it difficult for them to concentrate on their work.

The scientists responded by building sound-proofing around the animal laboratory so that the screams could not be heard.

PART THREE

STRATEGIES AND TACTICS

'All that is necessary for the triumph of evil is that good men do nothing.'
  Edmund Burke

INTRODUCTION

Although I am vehemently opposed to all aspects of animal cruelty this section of 'Fighting for Animals' is, for reasons which I explained at the start of this book, devoted to the subject of vivisection.

Morally there is no question that experimenting on animals is a vile business. Ethically, the vivisectors are in the position of slave traders, arms dealers and concentration camp guards. There is no possible excuse for what they do. So why do we allow these scientists to perform these foul experiments?

There are tens of thousands of anti-vivisection groups in existence around the world. Some of these groups have been in existence for a century. Millions of people want animal experiments stopped. And yet the experiments continue.

It is time to change our strategy and our tactics.

Sadly, we won't defeat the vivisectors simply by stating the facts. Most people simply don't want to know what goes on in the vivisectors' laboratories.

And I don't believe that violence is the answer. I can understand the feeling of frustration shown by those who argue that the vivisectors are cruel and inhuman. I realise that social and political change has often been forced through by those using violence. And I recognise that attacks on buildings have attracted attention to the whole question of vivisection. But I do not believe that bombing laboratories or shooting vivisectors will stop animal experiments. Indeed, I fear that such violence may lose us public support. And although I realise that most attacks are aimed at buildings and property I am worried that someone might be injured.

I believe that the battle to end vivisection will be won entirely through public opinion - and that means through the media. And I believe that we can - and will - win.

The vivisectors - who have huge financial resources behind them - have persuaded millions that animal experiments are essential and that people who want animal experiments stopped are simply animal loving nutters. A false perception - devised by the pro-vivisection movement - has won over reality. We have to fight a propaganda war. And we have to recruit more supporters each day. Above all we have to remember that this is a war about perception not reality.

Those of us who care must tell everyone we talk to that if they do nothing then they are just as responsible for what goes on in the vivisection laboratories as the vivisectors themselves. We must explain to the unconverted that animal experiments are done in their name and with their money and that anyone who does and says nothing is supporting the status quo - and that means supporting the vivisectors.

In order to win the war against vivisection we have to prepare a battleplan: we need to decide upon the strategy we will use. For decades the war against vivisection has been a disparate, disorganised affair; controlled emotionally rather than intellectually.

We have failed to win (or even make any noticeable progress) in this war against vivisection for two reasons.

First, the vivisectors and their supporters are in the strong position of being in control of the status quo. Politicians and public both resist change. Those who are in control of the status quo are always in a position of strength.

And second, we care too much. I don't suggest for a second that anyone opposed to vivisection should try to care any less. But because all anti-vivisectionists are emotionally involved - and desperately want to see this barbaric practice stopped - we have failed to analyse the problem properly.

We should have won by now. We have many advantages. For a start we try harder. Most anti-vivisectionists don't get paid but they don't go home at the end of the working day and forget about the battle. Many anti-vivisectionist have devoted their lives to this cause - and seen no real progress.

Our other big weakness is that because anti-vivisectionists as a group are caring, fair and reasonable people we have tried to fight a fair and reasoned war. But the vivisectionists lie and use every dirty trick they can find. We have to be a little more imaginative and creative if we are to defeat them.

The battle against vivisection has to be won and it has to be won sooner rather than later. I don't want to die knowing that the battle against vivisection still hasn't been won. We are the only hope the animals have.

The supporters of vivisection are not emotionally involved in what they do and so vivisection is defended coldly and coolly and without concern for what is right or what is wrong. Our opponents are defending a wealthy and powerful group: they use any methods available to them. They have, over the years, clearly decided that the most powerful weapon in their armoury is to claim that vivisection is essential to human health. With this as a weapon they rely on the selfishness and self interest of the average citizen to enable them to maintain the status quo. They dishonestly and ruthlessly claim that without animal experiments human lives will be at risk. This is the basis of the well known 'do you want your child to live or are you prepared to allow us to perform a trivial experiment on this anonymous laboratory rat?' argument which has proved so effective over the years. It is, of course, an entirely spurious and dishonest argument but that doesn't worry the vivisectors and their supporters; they will happily rewrite history and use any arguments available to them in order to protect the vivisection industry. The opposition knows only too well that perception is more important than truth.

In order to counter this sort of crude intellectual terrorism we must develop a policy of counter intellectual terrorism.

Since our opponents lie and play fast and loose with the truth we must be willing to counter their arguments in any necessary way. This is not a game. It isn't the taking part that matters. Winning the small arguments doesn't matter in the slightest. The only thing that matters is winning the war. If you believe that the principles of anti-vivisectionism are worth fighting for then you must be prepared to do whatever is legally, morally and ethically necessary to win.

The vivisectors have influence over those in power at the moment and we are the ones who have to create change. The system doesn't want change. We have to force change upon the system. We don't have to influence parliament (there are no laws to be repealed). We simply have to convince the public to put pressure on the companies who pay for animal experiments. This war is all about money. When drug and cosmetic companies (who are between them responsible for most animal experiments) realise that vivisection is costing them money they will test their products in other ways.

And there is one thought that should give us all extra hope and joy: once we stop animal experiments we know that no one will ever again be able to find a reason to reintroduce them.

Remember: we only have to win this war once.

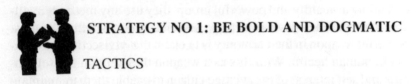 **STRATEGY NO 1: BE BOLD AND DOGMATIC**

TACTICS

Some anti-vivisectionists believe that we can't stop all animal experiments and that we should, therefore, aim to make progress against vivisection in small steps - campaigning for smaller cages, better conditions, fewer animals being used and so on. I think that this is a dangerous philosophy. If you start by asking for bigger cages there is a danger that in five years time you will regard it as an achievement when the vivisectors promise to make sure that all animal cages are painted in pleasant pastel colours. If you campaign for bigger cages, or the banning of the importation of animals from one or two specific countries, then there is a real danger that the public will feel that things can't be all that bad - and that vivisection must be necessary.

We will never get anywhere by being prepared to compromise and move forward in tiny steps - begging and pleading for improved facilities for animals. I believe that those who try to push for abolition the slow route are playing into the hands of the opposition. It is dangerous to compromise. The big hazard is that the steps forward will get smaller and smaller and the goal - abolition - will for ever remain out of reach. The vivisectors and their supporters will give in here a little and there a little but they will retain complete control of the situation. The prospect of vivisection stopping completely becomes a complete non starter if we take this attitude.

We should state our single aim simply and starkly: we want all animal experiments stopped. This is not a dream, it is a goal. If we don't actively campaign for abolition then we'll never get it. Have you ever heard of any campaigning group getting more than they campaign for?

In order to reach our goal we should be blunt, bold and dogmatic. We must insist that all animal experiments are useless, that no animal experiment has ever been of any value and that all animal experiments must be stopped.

We must not be afraid to be tough. We won't win this war without some degree of confrontation and without making enemies. Some anti-vivisectionists worry about upsetting the opposition. They believe that we should be conciliatory and try to win through negotiation. Well, stuff that. We will never, ever win through negotiation for the simple reason that the other side has too much to lose. Women didn't get the vote and slaves didn't win their freedom by negotiating behind closed doors. They made many enemies and fought long and hard for their rights. Laboratory animals can't fight for themselves so we have to fight for them. Remember what Lewis Carroll once wrote: 'If you limit your actions in life to the things that nobody can possibly find fault with you will not do much.' We will win more speedily if we aggravate the vivisectors and their supporters as much as we can.

The vivisectionists seem to regard those organisations who campaign for improvements in animal welfare as sensible, well mannered and worldly and this is surely warning enough. I would regard it as an insult if a vivisector thought I was reasonable. If the vivisectors don't hate and fear me then I can't possibly be doing any good.

We will achieve nothing without certainty and belief, conviction and commitment. This isn't a question of being over optimistic or unrealistic (as some anti-vivisectionists will argue) but of summoning up inner strength. We have to win because vivisection is wrong. And we need to be bold.

Some anti-vivisectionists fear that it is difficult to sustain the argument that no animal experiments are or ever have been of value. But it isn't. I have for years followed this simple 'black and white' theory; arguing that animal experiments are worthless, always have

106

been worthless and always will be worthless. (I have never lost a debate with a vivisector and for some time now vivisectors have refused to debate with me. I mention this because I think it proves the point most effectively: a dogmatic dismissal of animal experimentation can be sustained. The evidence needed to sustain this simple argument is available in my books *Why Animal Experiments Must Stop* and *Betrayal of Trust* - both published by the European Medical Journal.)

The truth is that if we let the vivisectors claim that progress has been made in any area of medicine then we will never win the war. The public will remain confused and we will never gain the public support we need. If we allow the vivisectors to argue that some experiments are of value (however slight) then we make it easier for the vivisectors. After all, how is anyone to know which experiments to abandon and which are worth doing? The vivisectors would argue that even if only one experiment in a million produces results of value then animal experiments must continue. We have to argue that the very unpredictability of the value of animal experimentation makes every experiment useless. The logic of our argument is unassailable. What is the point of doing any animal experiments if you never know whether the results are of value or not?

We can support our argument by using the evidence which shows that drug companies use this unpredictability to their advantage and happily ignore animal experiments which produce 'inconvenient' results. If animal tests show that a drug is safe the drug company concerned will use the tests to enable them to launch their new drug. But if the animal tests which are done show that a drug is unsafe the drug company will dismiss the tests as irrelevant - since they were done on animals!

 STRATEGY NO 2: FIGHT A PROPAGANDA WAR

TACTICS

Introduction
There are some anti-vivisectionists who insist on trying to fight the vivisection supporters simply with entirely accurate, scientifically valid statements. That is just not enough. It is like using bows and arrows to

fight an opposition armed with nerve gas. The opposition fights dirty. The vivisectionists have distorted the evidence so much that the truth is no longer sufficient and it is naive to imagine that it is.

This is a war not about reality but about perception. Our opponents have managed to convince large numbers of the population that animal experiments are essential for medical progress. There are millions of people who believe that if animal experiments stop then their children will be at risk.

'I like animals,' they say, 'and I dislike the idea of vivisection - I wouldn't like my daughter to marry a vivisector - but when it comes down to it I love my family more than I love animals.'

That belief is not inspired by reality but by a perception of reality; a perception that has been devised by the vivisectors and their supporters.

When we try to combat that belief by simply arguing that animal experiments are not relevant to human beings then the opposition merely repeat their claims that they are.

They deliberately highlight specific, small items out of the scientific literature since it is in their interest to bog the whole argument down in minutiae. They know that once we start arguing about scientific minutiae then we are lost: the public will get bored and stop listening.

We must be careful not to get dragged into lengthy public debates dealing with scientific minutiae since the result, in addition to boredom, will be confusion. When scientists start disputing history and nitpicking over scientific trivia the ordinary man in the street doesn't know who to believe. But on balance he worries more about his child and his family than he does about a bunch of anonymous animals so he remains a silent supporter of the status quo.

In order to combat the exaggerated nonsenses put forward by the vivisectors and their supporters we must aggressively trump their arguments in very public, unequivocal and dramatic ways.

Understand how the media work

Many anti-vivisectionists are extremely naive about the media. The vivisectionists use professionals who know how these things work. On the other hand most of the people who are fighting for animals are caring and sweet but sadly unsuspicious.

It is fairly widely understood that crowds tend either to destroy or to worship the object of their attention. And they can turn on a whim. The individual who is, at one moment, a hero can easily become a villain. It is less well understood that newspapers are much like crowds. They can turn a villain into a hero or a hero into a villain in the printing of a page.

A friend, a former editor of a newspaper, once told me a story which illustrated this fact well. Late one day the newspaper which he helped to edit received a story about a man. The details of the story are irrelevant. The newspaper's first inclination was to turn the man into a hero. They planned to publish a photograph and a story drawing the attention of their readers to the wonderful things this man had done. But as they planned their story another, even better story came into the newsroom. And the individual who was at the centre of this story was even more of a hero than the first person. And so, because the newspaper did not want to have two heroes on its pages, the editors turned the first man into a villain. A man who had, a moment or two earlier, been a hero in waiting now became a villain in waiting. He was attacked and vilified for doing the very same things for which, a moment or two earlier, they had been planning to praise him. And a man's life was ruined simply so that the newspaper editors could 'balance' the stories on their pages. Depending upon the way in which it is written virtually any individual can be described as both a hero and a villain.

The vivisectionists know this and they gladly feed newspapers and broadcasters with all the 'heros' and 'villains' they could possibly want. They will gladly lie and distort the evidence in order to win another point or two.

I have considerable first hand experience of this since the dishonest rumours about me never seem to end. They started some time ago, when I first started to campaign against the over prescribing of tranquillisers. A man whose name I cannot remember telephoned and wrote to numerous newspapers and television stations claiming that he was a tranquilliser addict and that I had been responsible for his predicament. I had, he claimed, been the doctor who had over prescribed pills for him. Quite a few journalists told me that they had heard this story. Since I had for many years campaigned against the over prescribing of tranquillisers the rumour did my reputation a considerable amount of harm. At one stage a newspaper for which I wrote decided to investigate the man's claims (at my suggestion). They asked him for more details. He named the town where I was supposed to have treated him and the year when I was supposed to have got him hooked on pills. It wasn't difficult to disprove his claim. I had never practised in the town he named. And in the year when he claimed that I had been over prescribing pills I had still been at school (ordinary school not medical school).

Since those early days the lies have become commonplace and ever more imaginative. I have, for example, lost count of the number of times that I have been told by journalists that they have been assured that since I do not have a medical degree I am not entitled to call myself 'Dr'. (In fact, I have a medical degree and an honorary science doctorate and I practised as a GP in the British National Health Service for a decade.) Vivisectionists work on the same philosophy as Adolf Hitler and his accomplices: if you tell a lie often enough and loudly enough it will become the truth.

Be Especially Wary Of Television

The vast majority of the stuff now made for television is superficial, trivialising crap put together by untalented dickheads with an average IQ smaller than a ballerina's shoe size.

I find it frightening to think that there are people who think the stuff they see on television is a true account of the state of the world.

To get a job as a television presenter these days you need a £30 haircut and a 50 pence brain. Anything that comes out of a TV presenter's mouth, looks like an ad lib and sounds vaguely witty will be the result of the efforts of a team of script writers.

When I was young and innocent I used to do a lot of television. But no more.

I lost most of my remaining faith in television when a producer told me that she wasn't going to broadcast an interview in which I had revealed the truth about a laboratory experiment for which a number of dogs had died because she had been reliably informed by the researchers that they hadn't used any animals at all.

'But I've got the evidence!' I protested. 'They published a re-search paper describing what they'd done.'

'But they didn't use any animals,' argued the producer. 'They only used animal tissue.'

What could I say to that? I'm proud of the fact that I managed to put the telephone receiver down without breaking it.

I was banned by one programme after I swore at someone on a late-night chat show.

Genuinely (and I still think quite reasonably) angered by the other guests I used a word rhyming with 'duck' but beginning with a letter coming a little later in the alphabet.

The word is heard constantly in films shown much earlier in the evening and it first appeared in The Times over a century ago, but the television company concerned was dismayed because I'd used it in anger.

I got stacks of mail and all the letters except one were con-gratulatory and supportive (the exception came from my mother) and as far as I know the TV company didn't receive any complaints, but the producer demanded a public apology which I refused to give.

I rather think that what upset them was not the use of the word itself but the fact that I'd used it in anger. I'd meant it. I'd spoken with passion and feeling.

After years of appearing on TV programmes I honestly feel that television producers don't feel entirely comfortable with passion. They don't really know how to deal with it. And it frightens them.

Television is a medium that has lost its way; it's part show business, part advertising billboard and part propaganda vehicle for politicians. Television promised much but has failed to deliver.

My advice is that you be extremely careful when dealing with television journalists. Most of them are not very bright. (The best journalists work for newspapers and the best of the best work for tabloid newspapers). People who work in television are easily influ-enced by the establishment and they are often unwilling to risk broad-casting anything which might prove to be controversial or trouble-some.

In particular, I suggest that you should try to avoid having any-thing to do with pre-recorded programmes. Just remember that any-thing you can say be turned against you and however sensible, and logical you may sound television journalists can make you look like a blithering idiot (at best) or a dangerous, homicidal maniac (at worst).

Learn To Influence Editors

In a column written for the Glasgow Evening Times in Scotland I wrote about the way animals are abused.

I pointed out that animals are treated abominably by the people who breed and kill them for a living and I warned readers that meat can cause cancer. The article was headlined: 'Death threats will not stop me speaking out'.

I wasn't surprised when the Meat and Livestock Commission (MLC) complained to the Press Complaints Commission (PCC). In asking the PCC for a ruling on my article the MLC said: 'The claims made in the article are both damaging to the industry and could be greatly disturbing to the public if given further publication.'

The PCC asked for evidence supporting my statement that: 'young people who eat meat are far more likely to get cancer and die young.' I supplied them with several pages of scientific references.

It seemed to me that it was important that as a columnist I should have the freedom to warn my readers of this evidence. However, the Press Complaints Commission found in favour of the Meat and Livestock Commission.

The PCC reported that the MLC: 'denied that there was any evidence to link the consumption of meat with the cause of cancer...' and in its judgement the PCC complained that my article contained 'no acknowledgement of any opposing view'.

The PCC was right about one thing. My original column about meat did not contain any 'acknowledgement of any opposing view'. It didn't seem to me to be necessary - the meat industry is perfectly capable of looking after itself - and it was pretty clear that in my column I was expressing my opinion.

* * * *

A short while later the Press Complaints Commission received a complaint from the Research Defence Society about one of my columns in The People newspaper.

The RDS made several specific complaints about a column I had written attacking vivisectors and the practise of vivisection.

In the column I had published evidence from America showing that pets may be stolen for use in laboratories, I had pointed out that I was convinced that animal experiments are of no value at all to human beings and I had estimated that vivisectors torture and kill 1,000 animals every 30 seconds. I had also stated that I believe that vivisectors torture animals for their own amusement or for professional gain.

The editor of The People, Bridget Rowe, made her position clear in a letter to the Press Complaints Commission. She wrote: 'Dr Vernon Coleman is well known as someone who feels very strongly about this issue. It is clear, by the very nature and layout of the column, that the column reflects his personal views and are not necessarily those of the newspaper. I therefore think that the Commission will be treading a very dangerous path should it uphold a complaint on the basis that it feels an opinion should not be held (no matter how unreasonable either the Commission or the complainant may feel that opinion is).'

Ms. Rowe pointed out that 'It would be, I fear, inappropriate for the Press Complaints Commission to enter into a debate as to who is right and who is wrong and to do so would stifle the very purpose of columns such as "Vernon Coleman".'

The Press Complaints Commission duly decided against the Research Defence Society's complaint - concluding that my attack on vivisection was not a breach of its Code.

The PCC decided that: 'readers would have been aware that in general the columnist was expressing his own strongly held views' and that: 'any overstatement, whether in statistics or otherwise, would have been understood as opinion or thought provoking exaggeration.'

(You may be amused to hear that I subsequently managed to include all the points about which the RDS had complained in a single sentence in my column. I thought this might make it easier for them to complain in future.)

* * * *

I mention these two incidents not because I was surprised that the Press Complaints Commission received these complaints but because of the unpredictability of the results. When I wrote a strongly opinionated column in the Evening Times I was found guilty by the PCC because I didn't put both points of view.

But when I wrote a strongly opinionated column in The People I was found not guilty by the PCC because I was expressing my own strongly held views.

For reasons which I confess I do not understand editors tend to regard the Press Complaints Commission very seriously. Lobby groups working for those who abuse animals know this. And so, as a fervent campaigner against animal cruelty, I attract a vast number of complaints. (My articles probably attract more complaints than any other journalist in the country. But very few of the complaints come from ordinary readers. Most come from lobby groups and public relations specialists operating on behalf of farmers, drug companies, vivisectors and others.)

Of course, editors often receive angry letters too. And the lobbyists know that a sternly worded 'letter to the editor' can be a powerful tool. Letters of complaint are written by eminent academics, representatives of national organisations, local doctors and spokesmen for local industries who disapprove of my articles because they are not good for business. In addition there are also frequently attacks from big lobbying groups working on behalf of vested interests. A letter of complaint does not have to prove an error or even a misinterpretation - it merely has to suggest that the author of the original article is a controversial figure and not someone well thought of by the establishment. The word 'controversial' seems to frighten many editors. I am often described as a controversial writer but all I ever do is tell the truth and the list of accurate predictions I have made is many pages long. I cannot recall any inaccurate predictions. It is a strange comment on our times that 'controversy' is too often regarded as a synonym for 'honesty' and that honesty is regarded a an unwelcome visitor on the pages of our newspapers; too rich a fare for the appetites of ordinary readers.

I am not in the slightest bit bothered by the Press Complaints Commission. They can huff and they can puff all they likes - I refuse to take any notice of them. If this results in my being fired then so be it. I would rather be fired than silenced. And I now regard being fired as merely a sign that I am being effective. But many journalists dare not risk being fired. And young journalists are likely to steer away from writing articles attacking vivisection when their newspapers receive nothing but complaints.

You can help in two ways.

First, if you ever see an article in a newspaper or magazine attacking vivisection do please send a letter of praise to the editor. Try to say something new and constructive. The editor and the journalist will be encouraged. Don't nit pick and don't whinge. If you can't find something really encouraging to say don't say anything at all. (It is common for my articles attacking vivisection to inspire numerous letters of complaint from people who describe themselves as anti-vivisectionists. A common complaint is that their particular group or organisation has not been mentioned.)

Second, if you see an article praising vivisection in any way send a letter to the editor putting the other point of view. And send a letter of complaint to the Press Complaints Commission. (If the editor of the newspaper or magazine doesn't print your letter you may be able to complain about that to the Press Complaints Commission too.)

Take Action Yourself

I regularly open envelopes from which fall small, undated newspaper cuttings and short typed notes. There is invariably nothing to show the name or the address of the newspaper from which the cutting has been taken. The notes are from readers instructing me to reply to letters supporting vivisection which have appeared in their local newspapers. The readers usually apologise for not giving their names or their addresses. The cutting consists of a letter from a representative of an organisation which supports and promotes vivisection and contains the usual arguments in favour of animal experimentation.

I receive letters and cuttings like this virtually every day of the week. In each case the reader, the person who has sent me the cutting, wants me to write a reply. They usually give two reasons for wanting me to reply. They argue that because my name is better known than theirs then if I send a letter there is a greater chance that the editor of the newspaper will print it. And they say that I will be better able to prepare a reply than they are. The first of these two assumptions is entirely false. The truth is that local newspaper editors are much more likely to publish letters which come from local readers than they are to publish a letter from someone, however well known, who writes from afar and is unlikely to be a reader, subscriber or advertiser. The second assumption is also untrue. Anyone who consults my book *Why Animal Experiments Must Stop* will be able to refute all the hoary old arguments put forward by the vivisectionists. And, of course, the more letters a campaigner writes the better the letters will become.

You may write five, ten, twenty, even fifty letters before you get one published. But you must not give up. As you put yet another stamp on yet another envelope you will suffer agonies of self doubt and you will wonder whether all the effort is worthwhile. It is. Remember that you are not the only person writing letters. Newspapers, magazines and TV and radio programmes all rely upon public support. No editor or producer can afford to ignore public demands. The constant barrage of mail will eventually persuade editors and producers to run features and programmes describing or at least outlining the horrors and uselessness of vivisection.

Remember that when writing to newspapers or magazines it is important not to get bogged down in too much detail. Keep your letters short - covering one or, at most, two sheets of notepaper. Remember that Voltaire once wrote 'To hold a pen is to be at war'. Don't waffle and before you write try to find out the full name (and qualifications and title) of the person you're writing to. Give your name and address and sign your letter. Simply state the facts - and your opinions. When a magazine or newspaper publishes an anti-vivisection letter write a letter of praise and support to the editor. Keep stating the facts and your opinions.

And if your letter is published and a pro-vivisectionist sends in a reply make sure that you reply to their letter and don't take it too much to heart if you find their response upsetting. Vivisectionists attack me frequently and I think it is a good sign. The German philosopher Arthur Schopenhauer stated that all truths go through three phases:

1. Ridicule

2. Violent opposition

3. Acceptance as being self evident.

We have recently moved into stage two - proof that we are having an impact.

Remember: when writing to newspapers always try to have the last word. And remember that there are far fewer vivisectionists than there are anti-vivisectionists. Let's keep them really busy - and stretched in every way.

It is undoubtedly much easier to stuff a cutting into an envelope and send it to me than it is to sit down and prepare a neatly argued 'Letter to the Editor' but if I replied to all the cuttings which are sent to me I would have no time for any other writing and at the end of it all my life would have been completely wasted for very few of my letters would have ever been published. I did once try to send letters in reply to all such cuttings - I sent off hundreds of letters a year - but I now send very few.

If all the people who claim to care about animals spent just ten minutes a day writing letters against animal experiments or some other barbarism then all these evils would be stopped within a year.

(This seems a good point to apologise to all those readers who write in asking me to answer complex questions about animal experimentation. I used to try to answer all such queries. But I can no longer do so. Many letters raise questions which I have dealt with at length in various books but demand lengthy, personal answers. When I do not provide the required answers some of the writers take offence. Some write indignantly and tell me that they are so peeved that they do not intend to do anything to help animals. But if I replied to all these letters I would never be able to do anything else to help the animals.)

Write A Book

If you have something to say then write a book. If you can't find a publisher then publish it yourself. It was the Central Intelligence Agency which stated: 'One single book can significantly change the reader's attitude and action to an extent unmatched by the effect of any other single medium.'

Make Sure Anti-Vivisection Publications Are In Public Libraries

Regularly visit your local library and check that the library has got copies of all the best anti-vivisection books and animal rights books. Take a list with you, tick off the ones that aren't on the shelves and hand the list to the librarian. This helps in several ways. First, and most important, it ensures that good anti-vivisection reading material is available for anyone who wants it. Second, it reminds the librarian that the animal issue is an important one. Third, it encourages publishers and authors to produce more pro-animal books. I don't know of anyone who has ever got rich writing animal rights books so don't worry that you'll simply be making other people rich. I know that I have to subsidise my animal rights books by writing other books. No commercial publisher would produce *Betrayal of Trust* for example and although it has reprinted several times and sold around 5,000 copies the advertising costs have meant that the book still hasn't covered its basic costs (and nor is it likely to since every time I sell another copy I put the money towards more advertisements). And although around 8,000 copies of the English edition of *Why Animal Experiments Must Stop* have been distributed I've lost a lot of money on the book (partly because I have bought advertisements which haven't covered the costs and partly because I have given away many of the books). If this book ever makes a profit (a possibility I consider extremely unlikely) I will simply use the money to print, promote and distribute more copies.

By helping to boost the sales of existing animal rights books you will help to ensure that new books get published. (Look at the imprints on most animal rights books and you'll find that they have been published by the authors. Big publishing houses aren't much interested in publishing animal rights books for the simple commercial reason that hundreds of thousands of people won't rush out and buy them.)

Just as importantly, ask the librarian if you can leave some animal rights literature on display. Vivisectionists, who get funding from the mega-rich international drug companies, flood schools, colleges and libraries with their literature. We have to do the same.

Publish Your Own Leaflets

If you can't find any anti-vivisection leaflets (or other animal rights leaflets) which you are happy about distributing why not try writing, editing and printing your own? Leaflets are relatively cheap to print these days.

One suggestion: don't include horrible pictures of tortured or dying cats or dogs on your literature. People won't look at the leaflets.

Instead, take a look at Plan 2000's leaflets. Most have a photograph of a beautiful kitten or puppy on the front. Look at the photographs in this book to see just how dramatic the juxtaposition of the right caption and the right photograph can be.

Encourage Others To Write

Recruit new soldiers for the animal rights army every day. The antivivisectionist movement needs a constant supply of new soldiers to help fight the propaganda war.

Tell everyone you talk to that if they do nothing then they are just as responsible for what goes on in the vivisection laboratories as the vivisectors themselves. Animal experiments are done in our name and with our money. Anyone who does and says nothing is supporting the status quo - and that means supporting the vivisectors. The vivisectors have influence over those in power at the moment and we are the ones who have to create change. The system doesn't want change. We have to force change upon the system.

Use The Advertising Standards Authority

In theory the Advertising Standards Authority sounds like a good idea. The public is exposed to a seemingly endless variety of commercial propaganda and if the susceptible and the naive are to be protected from exploitation the country needs a strong, independent watchdog capable of providing protection for innocent consumers from the most misleading and manipulative advertisers.

But is the Advertising Standards Authority the watchdog the country wants and needs?

The ASA is a private body, funded by a voluntary levy on display advertising and direct mail. In 1994 the ASA had an annual budget of around £2.5 million. The money is collected by a separate body, the Advertising Standards Board of Finance, which calls the 0.1% levy a 'surcharge'. Although there seems to be some confusion about this within the industry advertisers don't have to contribute if they don't want to.

Although it claims to safeguard the public I wonder how many complaints really come from ordinary people without an axe to grind or a vested interest to protect.

It is certain that quite a few of the complaints the ASA receives come from industry and pressure groups. One advertiser told me that he routinely complains about all his rivals to the ASA 'just to tie them up in bureaucracy'.

In 1994 the Research Defence Society (one of the organisations which defends the use of animals in experiments) made a number of complaints to the ASA about two leaflets produced by Plan 2000 - an anti-vivisection group which I founded. The ASA upheld most of the complaints.

I believe that when an organisation like the ASA makes judgements on controversial issues like animal experimentation it must be clearly and publicly seen to be totally and unquestionably impartial.

One of the Council members of the ASA when it upheld the complaints was Richard Bradley, vice chairman of L'Oreal (UK) Ltd., and vice chairman of the Cosmetics, Toiletry and Perfumery Association. The cosmetics industry does a lot of animal experiments.

I asked the ASA whether Mr. Bradley or the ASA felt that there was any conflict between his presence on the ASA Council and an ASA adjudication following complaints relating to the use of animals in experiments.

The Director General of the ASA refused to answer my question.

She said: 'We do not disclose the position taken by individual members of Council during meetings. You can be assured, however, that members of Council declare any interest that they have before an adjudication is made, and where necessary they withdraw from the discussion.'

When Paul Flynn Member of Parliament and member of Plan 2000, wrote about this issue to the ASA he received a reply from the chairman, the Rt. Hon. Lord Rodgers of Quarrybank.

Lord Rogers said: 'The decisions of Council are, of course, collegiate. I mean by this that they are decisions of Council as a whole. For this reason it would be quite wrong to refer to the views of any individual member. The principle, as you will appreciate, is exactly the same as applies to the Cabinet.'

Using the Cabinet as a comparison, although impressively grandiose, does not seem to me to be a particularly suitable analogy. Surely the ASA Council would be better compared to a jury?

Moreover, I found it odd that the ASA, a private body which claims to safeguard the public and which insists that advertisers prove their claims, should fail to give a more specific answer to such an important question. I felt that if Richard Bradley had declared an interest and withdrew when the complaint against the anti-vivisection leaflets was being heard then the ASA should have said so straight away - and provided supporting evidence.

In the end the ASA gave The People this statement:

'There are only two reasons why a council member would withdraw. Firstly, if the decision would affect his own company, and secondly, if the decision would affect a direct competitor. Neither circumstance applied in this instance, so Mr. Bradley sat on the panel as normal.'

My feeling is that because Mr. Bradley did not withdraw, some of those who passionately oppose the use of animals in experiments may feel that they - and the animals whose interests they represent - have not received a 'fair deal'. Are not Plan 2000 and the cosmetics industry competitors?

* * * *

In June 1995 the small publishing house I run received a letter telling us that someone had complained about an advertisement for two of my books. By the time the ASA wrote to us the advertisement had already been withdrawn for commercial reasons (it hadn't sold enough books and we replaced it with another advertisement which has proved much more successful).

The complainant challenged the advertisement in three ways.

First they challenged whether or not I was medically qualified, as the advertisement implied. This challenge was easily met with a photocopy of my medical degree diploma. It was the other two complaints which proved more puzzling.

They challenged us to substantiate an advertising claim that my book *How to Conquer Pain* 'is packed with practical information designed to help you control or banish pain for good'. And they also challenged us to substantiate this claim: 'Between a third and a half of all cancers may be caused by eating the wrong foods. In his best-selling book *Food for Thought* Dr Vernon explains which foods to avoid - and which to eat to reduce your risk of developing cancer.'

As evidence in our defence for *How to Conquer Pain* we offered the views of two entirely independent critics.

The Guardian reviewer had said: 'A clear and helpful handbook for pain sufferers. Perhaps most important of all is the way in which it brings pain down to a manageable level and gives self help ideas for sufferers.'

The Good Book Guide reviewer had said: '...this is a brilliant guide to understand and dealing with it (pain). It's written in plain language and well laid out to explain pain in general, different treatment approaches and an excellent personal pain management plan which covers both physical techniques (everything from drugs to rocking chairs) and mental attitudes'.

But we were told that the ASA will not accept what it calls testimonials. The ASA said: 'Book reviews do not constitute the kind of substantiation that is required.'

The ASA also said that the book itself: 'is unlikely to constitute acceptable evidence to the advertising claims as, we assume, it contains Dr Coleman's views, which are unlikely to constitute independent substantiation.'

So, in what seems to me to be a rather Kafkaesque situation, we found ourselves faced with trying to prove that the book is packed with information, with the rather large handicap of apparently not being able to use independent critics or the book itself.

We asked the ASA what they would consider to be acceptable evidence. Indeed, we asked them how they would set about proving that the Encyclopedia Britannica was 'packed with information' under their own conditions. They did not reply.

The ASA upheld the complaint.

The other complaint, which referred to my book *Food for Thought*, seemed easier to deal with. After all, books, official reports and scientific papers have all linked food and cancer. The United States Surgeon General has published a report suggesting that diet could be responsible for up to 70% of all cancers.

In order to support our claim that it is possible to reduce the risk of developing cancer by avoiding some foods and eating others we submitted a short but impressive list of basic references - referring to both books and scientific papers - and offered to provide a longer list if this was considered necessary.

But this time we hit another snag.

The ASA will not accept scientific references.

They had, they said, read the list of references. 'But', they added, 'this list in itself does not constitute evidence.'

We could not send original documents because much of the material had been obtained on loan from libraries and a telephone call to the Department of Trade and Industry confirmed our suspicion that it would be illegal (a breach of The Copyright, Designs and Patent Act of 1988) for us to provide the ASA with photocopies of all the books and scientific papers involved.

The ASA remained unmoved, simply insisting that: 'it is an advertiser's responsibility to submit all such evidence as is necessary to support their claims'.

We pointed out that back in 1990 the Health Education Authority reported that: 'diets containing plenty of fresh vegetables and fruit appear to have a protective effect in cancer of the stomach, oesophagus, large bowel and lung. Vegetable and fruit consumption should therefore be increased, especially fresh green and lightly cooked vegetables or salad'.

(We risked the copyright law and sent a photocopy of the relevant page of this report).

As a health writer who has spent 25 years fighting to reveal the truth about medicine and health matters I believe that it is vitally important to teach the public about the links between food and cancer.

But in February 1996 the ASA confirmed that they had recommended to their Council that the complaint about *Food for Thought* be upheld. (The original complaint was reported in June 1995.) They said that they: 'saw no convincing evidence that eating certain foods could prevent cancer, as implied by the advertisement.'

When I heard their conclusions I was sad, frustrated and angry. But not surprised.

After the Advertising Standards Authority ruled that the advertisement for my book *Food for Thought* was not allowable I wrote to the Minister at the Department of Health. I subsequently received a reply quoting the Health of the Nation White Paper from 1992. This stated: 'There is mounting, though inconclusive, evidence that diets low in meat and fat, and high in vegetables, starchy staple foods, cereals and fruits may be associated with a lower occurrence of cancers of the stomach and large bowel, breast, ovary and prostate. Obesity is also associated with an increased incidence of cancers of the gall bladder and uterus, and increased fatality from breast cancer in later life.'

There is more than a little irony in the fact that I get into trouble with the Advertising Standards Authority. I constantly refuse to have anything at all to do with any commercial products. I will not use whatever reputation I may have to sell any product (apart from the books which I write). And I have, for many years, fought hard against advertisers whose messages I have found unfair, misleading or potentially dangerous!

The ASA is not an organisation with which I am impressed but whatever your own feelings may be I suggest that every time you see an advertisement supporting or defending vivisection you make a complaint to the Advertising Standards Authority - and ask all your friends to complain too.

STRATEGY NO 3: INVOLVE THE PUBLIC

TACTICS

Tell People That Vivisection Is Worthless - But Don't Frighten Them

Many enthusiastic anti-vivisectionists put a lot of effort and time and money into finding yet more evidence to show that animal experiments are barbaric. Courageous anti-vivisectionists frequently work 'undercover' in laboratories and emerge with yet more horrifying evidence. Sadly, I do not think that these efforts are worthwhile. I honestly do not feel that the anti-vivisection cause needs any more evidence showing that animal experiments are barbaric. If that sort of evidence was going to help us win the war against vivisection we would have won long ago.

We have failed to win solely because the vivisectors are very good at persuading the public that what they do is essential and worthwhile. They have become adept at trumping our moral arguments with their pseudo-scientific arguments.

Their dishonest propaganda works solely because if you keep repeating something often enough it will eventually be perceived as the truth. The Nazis used a similar propaganda technique.

Vivisection is big business (it is the foundation of the world's largest and most profitable industry) and vivisectionists will lie and cheat to win. A vivisectionist once confessed to me that although they know that vivisection has absolutely no medical value they have to claim that it has in order to persuade the public to continue to support them. He admitted that the public view is that vivisection is such a vile business that unless there is some sound justification for it then it would soon be stopped. 'Only by convincing people that what we do saves human lives can we persuade them to support us with money,' he admitted.

If we want to stop animal experiments then we must make sure that the public know the truth: that animal experiments are danger-ously misleading and entirely unnecessary. Explain that drug side ef-fects are a consequence of animal experiments - and point out to a potential recruit that they and their family and friends will be safer if all animal experiments can be stopped. Vivisectors and their support-ers (who never let the truth interfere with their claims) often argue that animal experiments help save human lives. That isn't true. Animal experiments are of absolutely no value to human beings. No one would dream of trying out drugs intended for sheep by giving them to cats or goldfish or horses and expecting to get sensible results so why on earth do scientists expect to get any sensible results by trying out treatments intended for humans on rats, dogs, mice and other ani-mals? The whole business of animal experimentation isn't just mor-ally and ethically indefensible: it is also scientific and medical lunacy.

The vivisection supporters will often claim that if animal ex-periments are stopped then medicine will stop making progress. They make all sorts of absurd claims for the work the vivisectors do. They threaten and frighten ordinary people. They claim that people must choose between animals and their children. They win the support of some members of the public by telling them that animal experiments will help find a cure for the disease from which they or a member of their family are suffering. This is intellectual terrorism of the very worst sort; it is cold, calculated cruelty.

The harsh and undeniable truth is there are scores of drugs on the market which are known to cause cancer or other serious problems when given to animals (there is a list of such drugs in my book *Betrayal of Trust*). If you ask those drug companies why they sell medicines which are known to cause serious problems when given to animals they will tell you that animals are different to people - and that it is impossible to use animal experiments to predict exactly what will happen when a drug is given to a human patient!

Drug companies know very well that if they tested their products properly most of their new drugs would never get onto the market. They would lose billions of pounds. And so they use animal experiments to get their new drugs on the market.

What the vivisectors do not tell people is that virtually all the drugs which have been taken off the market because they cause serious problems when given to human beings were originally tested on animals and approved as safe

* * * *

Because the ordinary man, woman and child in the street are important it is vital that we do not alienate them.

We must be careful not to show people anything which is too shocking or too frightening. If we publish pictures of animals in a laboratory we will put people off. They will turn over the page or throw the leaflet away in horror and disgust.

Publishing too many gory details about experiments has the same result. Everyone knows that horrible things go in laboratories. It is enough to hint at the horrors, rather than to provide really sickening pictures or stories. A picture of a fluffy bunny or cuddly kitten, allied to a brief description of what a vivisector might do to the animal is far more likely to be effective than a picture of a cat with electrodes sticking out of its head or a picture of a rabbit with red, inflamed and obviously sore eyes. Those photographs obtained by undercover agents are, I fear, unlikely to be of any real value in the fight against vivisection. I believe that the effort, energy and money currently being spent on finding yet more evidence of the barbaric nature of vivisection would be far better spent on spreading the word about the evidence which is already available. We have more than enough evidence available to show that what the vivisectors do is barbaric, senseless and entirely without value (apart from to the pharmaceutical industry). Besides, the reality is of little or no consequence. As the vivisectionists know only too well the only thing that matters is perception.

Most people will, if given the facts, come down firmly on our side. Given the fact that there are not all that many psychopaths around this is, perhaps, not all that surprising. Most people love animals. A survey in America showed that 28% of pet owners would ignore orders to evacuate their homes in the event of nuclear war if they were told that they had to leave their animals behind. In order to recruit more supporters we need only to give the bare facts - and to be dogmatic.

If the person you are talking to says that they don't have the time or the money to do anything tell them that you would prefer them to be honest to you and to themselves and admit that they don't care enough to do anything. You may lose a former friend. But you may gain a new supporter for the anti-vivisection movement. And do you really want to be friends with someone who cares so little about something that is so important? Think of yourself as a pebble thrown into a pond. The ripples you can produce will start more people thinking and talking about animal experimentation. If you can convert one new person a month to our campaign and they, in turn, then recruit one new person a month to the campaign, you will, in a very short space of time, have created your own army of supporters.

Remember: we must never be afraid to tell the truth and to announce with confidence and certainty that all animal experiments are worthless. The general public will only join us in large numbers when they realise that animal experiments are entirely without value.

Use This Simple Quiz To Help Recruit More Supporters

Ask the uncommitted to try this simple quiz - answering YES or NO to each question.

1. Do you like animals?

2. Do you agree animals suffer pain and distress if they are hurt or frightened?

3. Do you agree that if a kitten was ill it would be more sensible to treat it with a medicine which had been tested on other kittens than

with a medicine which had been tested on cows?

4. Do you agree that medical treatments should be as free as possible from side effects?

5. If you needed an operation would you rather the surgeon had experience of operating on other human beings rather than on cats, dogs or mice?

6. Do you agree that needless cruelty to animals should be stopped?

7. Would you be prepared to pay an extra few pence for drugs which you knew were less likely to cause serious side effects (or even kill you) because they had been properly tested rather than being tested on animals?

8. Would you be shocked to know that the animals used in laboratories include pets?

9. Do you agree that if animals are like people they should be treated with the same respect as people?

10. Do you agree that if animals are unlike people there is little point in using them to test drugs and procedures intended for people?

Score one point for every YES answer and no points for every NO answer. Tell the person doing the quiz that if they scored 1 or more points they are clearly a caring, sensitive, intelligent human being. You should then be able to recruit them to the anti-vivisection movement.

Whenever Possible Refer To Animals As He Or She

When people talk about other people they usually refer to them as 'he' or 'she'. The use of the sexually defining pronoun helps to identify, and give some personality, to the individual. But when vivisectionists talk about animals they usually refer to them as 'it' or 'them'. This deindividualisation is encouraged by the meat industry, the vivisectors and the hunters who are all intelligent enough to realise that their actions will be less defensible if animals are regarded as individuals.

Involve Organisations Of Which You Are A Member

If you are a member of any organisation which could conceivably have any interest in abolishing animal experimentation make your voice heard and get your organisation to commit itself. Remember: you do not have to recruit every member of your organisation in order to influence 'official policy'. Most major decisions are made by a tiny minority of organisation members - the rest will usually go along with whatever has been decided.

You may be unlikely to be able to get your local football, cricket or golf club committee to get involved in opposing animal experiments but if you are a member of a Women's Institute or religious group then there is an excellent chance that you will be able to convince other members that the organisation ought to make a public stance on the issue. You will probably need to influence only between 5% and 10% of the organisation's membership in order to get a resolution heard and passed.

Boycotts Work

Go into your local pharmacist or supermarket and ask to speak to the manager. Tell him that you do not intend to patronise his store until he stops selling products which have been tested on animals.

If there is a local charity shop find out if the charity does or supports animal experiments. If it does then tell the manager that you intend to call for a boycott of the shop. Try to get friends to call in or telephone with the same message. If you can get a few friends to make placards you could stand outside the shop and try to persuade others not to use it. Write to your local newspaper and tell them what you are doing. You may find that they will be interested in the story (especially if you can find some local celebrity or someone photogenic - e.g. a child, a local beauty queen or someone very old - to join you). If you can't get your local newspaper to run a news story about what you are doing write them a letter. If you cannot afford a stamp take the letter into the local newspaper office yourself.

Recruit Celebrities

Write to your favourite celebrities. Celebrity supporters are important because they help to attract public attention - and more support from fans - as well as media interest. Write to your favourite TV, film or pop star and ask them if they'll support the campaign to abolish animal experiments.

Speak Out In Public

Contact local schools, colleges, clubs etc. and ask them if you can go along and talk about the campaign to stop animal experiments. Explain that stopping vivisection is important to people as well as animals. If the organiser wants to invite someone from the 'other side' welcome the opportunity for a debate.

Here are some tips for speaking in public (including radio and television):

● Do not be afraid to be passionate - genuine passion (and it must be genuine) is exciting, eye-catching and seductive. Most professional television presenters are trained to hide their emotions and feelings. It is often argued that hot passion can look forbidding and even alarming on television - which is watched in the living room, kitchen and bedroom. The result is that real passion is rare these days.

● The experts will tell you that you must dress conservatively if you are appearing in public (whether on the stage or on television). The theory is that if you look as if you are part of the establishment then the people watching you will have faith in what you have to say. I think this was probably true ten years ago. But I don't believe it is true today. Most people have grown cynical about 'the men in suits'. They distrust politicians, official spokesmen and (by extension) any public speaker wearing a smart, dark suit, white shirt and expensive tie. As long as it is clean you can wear anything that you feel comfortable in. In fact there is an unexpected advantage to be gained from wearing clothes in which you feel comfortable. If you wear a suit which you associate with stressful situations (job interviews, important social occasions etc.) then you will feel stressed and uptight the moment you put it on. But if you wear casual, comfortable clothes you'll feel relaxed and casual. Looking relaxed and casual will help make you look honest and trustworthy.

● Find out beforehand how long you are likely to be expected to speak for. What sort of audience is likely to be listening to you? Who else is likely to be speaking with you? Who is likely to ask you questions? What questions are they likely to ask you?

● Whenever you speak in public always assume that everyone there is out to 'get you'. Don't trust interviewers, researchers or producers who are charming and apparently on your side beforehand. They are deliberately trying to relax you. The nicer they are the more likely they are to go for the jugular.

● If an interviewer is very aggressive and you feel cornered turn the tables on him by asking him (or her) why he (or she) feels the need to be so aggressive. If you can remain calm then do so. If your interviewer is cross and aggressive and you are calm, polite and gentle - and you constantly try to help him understand what you have to say - then you will almost certainly win the hearts of the audience. On rare occasions - for example, if other people on the programme will not answer your questions or if the interviewer is consistently rude and hectoring - you can get cross and show your anger. A display of passionate anger can be a good way of letting the audience know how you feel.

● Prepare what you are going to say - but if you are speaking or lecturing to a live audience try not to rely too heavily on a script and if you are appearing on television don't take a sheaf of notes in with you and expect to be able to have time to refer to them. If you must take in documents to which you intend to refer make sure that they are clearly labelled and that any passages you intend to quote are clearly marked with a highlighter.

● If you are being interviewed for television, radio or a newspaper you must be prepared for the fact that most journalists will think you are a complete nutter. The vivisectors (or, more accurately, those who support them and stand to benefit financially from the work they do) have successfully managed to portray anyone who opposes the use of animals in experiments as someone who loves animals more than human beings. Some journalists freelance in their off duty hours for drug companies and drug company sponsored journals and magazines. Journalists tend (as a rule) to be rather cynical, establishment orientated and right wing (even the ones working for apparently left wing, liberal and even apparently eccentric publications). They consistently show a natural tendency to believe what they are told by the establishment spokesmen and to distrust anything they are told by people who want to change the status quo.

● Do not agree to take part in debates in which the ground is uneven. The vivisectors will want to make up their own rules, controlling the nature and constitution of the audience and who will be chairman. There have even been occasions when the vivisectors have tried to choose the chairman and which members of the audience would be allowed to vote at the end of the debate!

Demonstrate Against Celebrities Who Support Vivisection

If you find that a celebrity or member of the royal family is a patron or member of a charity which performs or supports animal experimentation campaign against them when they are making a public appearance.

Draw Attention To The Medical Dangers Of Animal Experimentation: Remind People That Animal Experiments Kill People Too

Point out that by allowing drug companies and other scientists to perform animal experiments the public are endangering human lives. Doctor induced disease is a common and major problem. We can blame this epidemic of doctor induced disease on the use of animal experiments. (You will find more evidence for this argument in my book *Betrayal of Trust*). Four out of ten patients who are given pills will suffer noticeable, painful or even life threatening side effects. But few of the patients who suffer side effects realise that they are suffering because drug companies and doctors are allowed to test drugs on animals!

Pharmaceutical companies love to test drugs on animals because they can't lose. If the animal tests show that the drug doesn't produce side effects in animals the company will proclaim the drug 'safe' and put it on the market. But if the animal tests show that the drug causes side effects the company will dismiss the results as irrelevant - and put the drug on the market anyway - because animals are different to people!

When discussing animal experiments with friends point out that if they have ever suffered unpleasant side effects the chances are high that the drug they were given was tested on animals. And tell them that they are lucky to be still alive.

Here are three case histories (taken from my book *How To Stop Your Doctor Killing You*) which show that animal experiments kill people:

● Eight year old Samantha loved ballet dancing passionately. She wanted to be a ballet dancer when she grew up. But she never did grow up. Ten days before her ninth birthday she fell ill. Her ballet class was holding a public performance on the following Saturday and she desperately wanted to be well enough to appear so her mother took her along to see their family GP. Within 48 hours Samantha was dead: killed not by the illness but by the drug she'd been given. The drug had been tested but most of the early tests had been done on animals. These had not shown the side effect which killed Samantha.

● Forty four year old Robert failed a routine life assurance examination, carried out so that he could take out a new and larger mortgage on a house he and his wife had bought. He felt well but his doctor insisted on treating him. The drug he was given had been extensively tested on mice and rats. Unexpected side effects produced by the drug resulted in his death three weeks later.

● Bill was in pain. Doctors recommended surgery. The surgeon he saw wanted to try out a new technique that had been tested on animals. Bill died three days after the operation. He developed problems and complications which had not occurred when the operation had been performed on animals.

All these human tragedies occurred as a direct result of animal experiments. In all these case histories the identifying facts have been changed to protect the privacy of the families concerned. It isn't only animals who suffer from 'animal testing'. People suffer too.

Remember: no animal experiment has ever saved a human life, but animal experiments have resulted in many deaths.

Point Out That Doctors Agree With Us

A year or two ago I conducted what was, I believe, the largest survey of doctors ever published on the subject of vivisection. It may still be the largest such survey. I questioned five hundred British doctors to find their attitudes towards vivisection. The doctors were invited to agree or disagree with four statements and the following results were obtained. The survey was reported in the European Medical Journal and other journals.

●   Laboratory experiments performed on animals can be misleading because of anatomical and physiological differences between animals and humans.

88% agreed.

●   I would like to see scientists trying harder to find alternatives to animals for testing drugs and cosmetics.

81% agreed.

●   Patients would suffer fewer side effects if new drugs were tested more extensively on human cell and tissue cultures.

51% agreed.

●   Too many experiments on animals are performed.

69% agreed.

The vivisectionists do not like this survey but, to my surprise, very few anti-vivisectionists ever seem to bother to quote it.

Publicise The Horrors About The Way Animals Are Kept

Publicising the horrendous conditions under which animals are kept can be helpful. Again, photographs of the animals in cages are not necessary and may, indeed, be counterproductive since they are likely to distress members of the public.

Earlier in the book (page 95) I listed the official figures for the amount of floor space animals are allowed in laboratories

Encourage People To Write To Politicians

Some anti-vivisection organisations put an enormous amount of effort into trying to persuade political representatives to support their aims. A good deal of lobbying goes on and around the world there are many anti-vivisectionists who spend their days dressed in suits attending and preparing for committee meetings. I spoke at the House of Commons in London in December 1993. My speech didn't go down too well for I produced a lot of embarrassing evidence which proved quite conclusively that animal experiments are of absolutely no scientific or medical value. When I'd finished someone stood up and said that they wished that a representative from one of the reputable anti-vivisection groups had given the address. I got the impression that I had made some people feel uncomfortable by boldly breaking the negotiating rules by arguing for total abolition.

Negotiating with the enemy is, in my view, an entire waste of time. We will never ever win this battle behind closed doors. There is no room for negotiation. The bald truth is that no one has ever changed the status quo - and defeated huge vested interests - by negotiating behind closed doors. Our opponents love meetings, of course. They can enter into long, drawn out negotiations over cage size and so on in an attempt to convince us that they share our general aims, knowing full well that they will never have to do anything very dramatic at all. In my view there is no point at all in wasting time and energy being nice to or negotiating with the men in suits. Slavery wasn't abolished through gentle lobbying. Women didn't get the vote through sensible, reasoned discussions. South African blacks didn't win freedom by politely sitting down around a table with their oppressors.

Even if one believed that it would be possible to achieve abolition through negotiation there would still be no excuse for wasting time and energy negotiating with politicians.

The activity is entirely pointless and unnecessary for there are no laws requiring drug or cosmetic companies (or anyone else for that matter) to do animal experiments.

Many of those who advocate or defend animal experimentation claim that animals must be used before drugs or cosmetics can be put onto the market. Vivisectors - many of whom work for drug and cosmetic companies - often claim that they only do experiments because they are forced to do so by law. Many independent commentators and anti-vivisection supporters have been taken in by these claims but these claims simply are not true. The Home Office in the United Kingdom has confirmed to me that there are no laws - in Britain or the European Union - which require drug or cosmetic companies to perform animal experiments.

• *'There is no European Community or United Kingdom law which states that drug and cosmetic companies have to test their products on animals.'* (Baroness Denton of Wakefield CBE, Parliamentary Under-Secretary of State for Consumer Affairs and Small Firms)

• *'There is no European Community or United Kingdom law which states that drug companies have to test their products on animals.'* (Charles Wardle MP, Parliamentary Under Secretary of State, Home Office)

The absence of any law requiring drug or cosmetic companies to perform animal tests means:

a) No law will have to be repealed before animal experiments can be stopped.

b) Since it has now been proved that animal experiments are useless they can easily be stopped without parliamentary intervention.

c) Since drugs and cosmetics must obviously be tested before being sold the onus is now on drug and cosmetic companies to find effective ways of testing their products.

Since there are no laws requiring animal experimentation and there are no laws to repeal the behind closed doors discussions are a complete waste of time. However, I do believe that it is well worthwhile individuals writing to their political representatives in order to make sure that they are aware of the views of the voters.

Remember: politicians only ever respond to public opinion. They react rather than act. And they are also likely to respond well if they receive a letter from a constituent - a potential voter - telling them that a pledge to campaign for animals will gain a vote.

It is better to keep letters short since politicians won't read lengthy, boring, ranting letters. Don't get bogged down with minutiae. Just state the facts: boldly and with confidence. If you get an unsatisfactory reply then write again explaining why you consider the answer unsatisfactory. You should send letters not only to your own political representative but also to leading politicians in all political parties. You can obtain an up to date list of suitable recipients for your mail from your local public library. Letter writing can be extremely fruitful. In the summer of 1994 I wrote to all Members of Parliament in the British House of Commons. Within ten days I had received over 100 replies - with more than 60 MPs agreeing to support a campaign for complete abolition of animal experiments by the year 2000.

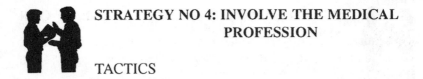

STRATEGY NO 4: INVOLVE THE MEDICAL PROFESSION

TACTICS

Attack Doctors

The quickest way to attract the attention of the medical profession is to go on the offensive - and to tie doctors in with the horrors of animal experimentation.

The role of the medical profession in the vivisection war has been vital but largely passive. The vast majority of doctors have nothing whatsoever to do with animal experiments. They have no idea what goes on. They are told (occasionally) that animal experiments are an essential part of the process by which new drugs are developed - and they believe that.

Those who support animal experimentation claim that they have the support of the medical profession (and will from time to time wheel out the odd medical supporter) but the truth is that most doctors are uninterested in what goes on.

I suspect that one way to attract the support of the medical profession for the anti-vivisection campaign may be to emphasise the danger done by doctors to patients (four out of ten patients who take a drug suffer an uncomfortable and in some cases potentially lethal side effect and one in six patients in hospital are there because they have been injured by a doctor) and to then (fairly) blame those problems on the use of animal experiments. This will give doctors an explanation and an excuse for doctor induced illness. Eventually doctors will leap on this excuse with enthusiasm and will become strongly antagonistic towards animal experimentation.

I feel that by highlighting the problems caused by doctors and then making sure that those problems are linked, in the public eye, with the use of animals in experiments we will force the medical profession to publicly oppose vivisection (Once again, there is more information supporting this argument in my book *Betrayal of Trust*.)

 STRATEGY NO 5: TAKE ADVANTAGE OF OUR SUPERIOR NUMBERS

TACTICS

Introduction

Every cause must use its strengths if it is to win. Our strength lies in the number of people who are opposed to animal experimentation.

Our problem is that the vast majority of those who want animal experiments to stop do not do enough. And the reason for this is that most people just don't care enough to make the effort. They will sign a petition or make a telephone call to a phone vote line because it costs virtually nothing and takes hardly any time. They may even buy a T shirt, wear a badge or join an organisation to convince themselves and others that they are caring, compassionate beings.

But although they may be disgusted and horrified by what goes on in laboratories up and down the country they will not put themselves out. And that is why we live in a society which is controlled by a seemingly endless procession of corrupt and incompetent governments.

We can all make a difference. If we make the effort. If you choose not to then you must bear the responsibility. If you don't fight for the things you believe in then what is the point of living? Unless you have something for which you would die where is the joy in being alive?

If 30, 20 or 10 million people did something every day to help the animals then the animals would soon all be saved.

We Must Unite

History is written by winners. We will win our battle against the vivi-sectionists. We are morally right. We are ethically right. We are medi-cally right. We are scientifically right. But we will not win until we are even more coordinated or determined than our opponents.

The vivisectionists lie, cheat and threaten as one. It is a tragedy that the anti-vivisectionists spend much of their energy fighting one another.

The disagreements between anti-vivisection groups are not usu-ally about policy so much as about personality. It seems to me that some of those who become actively involved in the campaign to stop animal experiments need to feel important. It is their own vanity which drives them to sit on committees (a peculiar activity at the best of times and something which I have managed to avoid since I was about nineteen). Vanity is a perfectly sound reason for doing things as long as you recognise that you are doing things because you are vain and you don't allow the reason to influence your actions.

The damaging dissent and internal strife which is such a fea-ture of the anti-vivisection movement is not peculiar to those who oppose animal experimentation. It is common among all groups who are driven by passion and a sense of righteousness. People who work within any movement always seem to be exceedingly critical of others within the same movement. When I was battling to stop doctors over-prescribing tranquillisers I was constantly stabbed in the back by peo-ple who claimed to want doctors to stop over-prescribing tranquillis-ers. It is, however, within the anti-vivisection movement that the point-less but damaging in fighting reaches the most spectacular levels.

Fired by a mixture of emotions individuals and groups who claim to be opposed to the use of animals in experiments spend most of their time fighting other anti-vivisectionists, rather than the vivisec-tionists.

I have always said that although I want all animal experiments to be stopped I would not attack or argue with anyone who was at least moving in the same direction. I have, for example, illustrated the point by saying that I would not campaign against or criticise some-one who only wanted to stop animal experiments on Wednesdays -even though I would obviously prefer everyone to campaign for a complete ban on all animal experiments (and, indeed, all abuse of animals).

Like other committed anti-vivisectionists I receive a constant barrage of mail from individuals who claim to be anti-vivisectionists but who seem to spend most of their time criticising other anti-vivisectionists, often putting forward points of view which one might expect to come from vivisectionists and their supporters.

In my view some of these back-stabbing individuals, self-centred megalomaniacs who are full of malice and spite and seem to have a greater love for themselves and their own reputations than for the animal kingdom, do more harm than the vivisectors. Their criticisms are never important or really relevant but the amount of time and effort they waste is colossal. They find something to moan about in everything that is written or said about vivisection. These individuals never do anything practical to help. They never seem to be around when a thousand envelopes have to be sealed, addressed and stamped or when a fund raising stall has to be manned. They don't spend time exposing vivisectors, risking legal action or taking on the establishment; instead they back-stab other anti-vivisectionists and spend time and money on empire building and self glorification. I very much doubt if they have any idea how difficult it is to fight the medical establishment, the drug industry, the politicians and the media (which are, by and large, disinterested in animal rights and opposed to the anti-vivisection movement). The worst thing these people do is to cause many would be supporters to abandon the anti-vivisection movement in despair. I am sad to have to say that I have been lied about, slandered and libelled as much by other alleged anti-vivisectionists as by vivisectors and their supporters. Most simply repeat and help to perpetuate the lies told by the vivisectionists. It is sometimes difficult to tell who is on which side.

For a long time I have been convinced that if the anti-vivisection movement had worked together then vivisection would have been stopped years ago.

At one point I made a real effort to bring together all the different anti-vivisection groups in the world, pointing out that the vivisectors work together to protect one another and that we would stand a much greater chance of winning our battle if we stood together too. Sadly, the attempt was a dismal failure.

STRATEGY NO 6: ATTACK VIVISECTORS

TACTICS

Introduction

Vivisectors are widely revered. But they do not deserve it. Most of them are blinkered, ignorant and not very bright. Many people assume that vivisectors are clever because they talk of incomprehensible things in an incomprehensible way. This is a big mistake. Plumbing gurgles loudly but there isn't necessarily any sense behind the gurgling. Our society needs vivisectors like it needs dry rot.

Isolate Vivisectors From Other Scientists

Make sure that you always refer to vivisectors as scientists (and never as doctors - which the vast majority of them are not). Already, a growing number of scientists make sure that members of the public know that they do not use animals in their research when talking about their work. By using the word scientists when talking about vivisectors you will be helping to give scientists in general a bad name. They will then fight even harder to disassociate themselves from the vivisectors. This, in turn, will mean that the vivisectors will gradually become isolated in a scientific, cultural and financial ghetto.

Do Not Treat Them With Respect

If you find yourself face to face with a vivisector do not treat him or her with respect. I have frequently come face to face with vivisectors and been expected to shake hands with them. I always refuse. On one occasion a television producer introduced me to a vivisector before a programme started and invited us to shake hands. I refused. Why would I want to shake hands with a vivisector? After the programme ended the producer wanted me to have a drink with the vivisector (and the other guests). Again, I refused. I explained that I had not been arguing against vivisection to help make an interesting programme but because I fervently believe that vivisection must be stopped.

Ridicule Them

Here is a short piece which I included in my newspaper column. It may give you some ideas:

'My articles about animal experimentation have been officially condemned by men in white coats for being too one sided. The Bureaucratic Society For Protecting Evil Bastards In White Coats Against Dangerous Columnists (BSFPEBIWCADC) has formally instructed me to put the other point of view. So here are ten great discoveries made by scientists experimenting on animals. After details of each experiment I have included a short note explaining how the research may help you and your family.

1. Baby monkeys get terribly upset when they are parted from their mothers and kept in solitary confinement in steel containers for long periods. (Shows that school children should not be kept in solitary confinement in steel containers).

2. Putting balloons inside animals' brains and blowing up the balloons causes brain damage. The bigger the balloon the greater the brain damage. (Clearly shows that children should not be allowed to blow up balloons inside each other's brains. And that big balloons are even more dangerous than small ones)

3. Rabbits' eyes go red and become sore and irritated when they are deliberately filled with toxic chemicals. (Suggests that you should not be surprised if your eyes hurt if you drop toxic chemicals into them).

4. Dogs die if they are forced to eat large quantities of soap. (Clear evidence that eating large quantities of soap is unwise).

5. Live pigs suffer severe burns when they are exposed to naked flames. (Shows that if you want to avoid severe burning you should keep your distance from naked flames).

6. If you shoot cats in the head they cry and scream a great deal, bleed a lot and then eventually die. (Suggests that shooting people in the head may be very noisy and messy.)

7. If you deprive guinea pigs of water for long periods they become very dehydrated and eventually die. (Clear support for the belief that humans who don't drink fluids will die.)

8. Puppies and other animals die when you remove essential organs such as kidneys. (Suggests that it is unwise to allow anyone to remove your kidneys).

9. Cats get very upset if you drill holes in their brains and then squirt chemicals into the holes. (Shows that drilling holes in peoples brains and then filling the holes with chemicals is anti-social).

10. Monkeys die when deliberately infected with bugs which cause fatal diseases in monkeys. (Shows that scientists who perform experiments on animals are all psychopathic dickheads).'

Create Vivisector Jokes

Question
How many vivisectors does it take to experiment on a mouse?
Answer
Thirty seven. One to hold the knife and thirty six to carry the drug company money to the bank.

Remind The Public That Vivisectors Are The Violent Ones

Vivisectors have worked hard to convince members of the public that all anti-vivisectionists are dangerous revolutionaries. The truth is, of course, that it is the vivisectors who are the violent ones. It is vivisectors who torture and kill the innocent.

Vivisectors Should Be Named

Animal rights organisations which fight against vivisection sometimes refuse to name vivisectors.

However, I am not convinced that we should protect the privacy of vivisectors.If we knew that Dr Mengele, the Nazi concentration camp "Angel of Death", was at work in a community hospital in our midst would journalists and campaigners refuse to name him - or the hospital where he was working - in order to protect his reputation and his well being? I hope not. The truth is the truth is the truth is the truth. And if the truth causes embarrassment for the vivisectors that is their problem. It is our duty to expose the evils of vivisection.

AFTERWORD

Vivisection is done in your name with your money. You have a right and a responsibility to speak out against it. Every night, before you go to bed, ask yourself this simple question:

'What have I done today to help the animals and to help stop the evil practice of vivisection?'

And remember: once stopped vivisection will never start again (it is so obviously unjustifiable). Our descendants will regard vivisection as an evil practice and will be astonished that we allowed it to continue for as long as we did.

Also available by Vernon Coleman

Why Animal Experiments Must Stop

Dr Coleman analyses the pro-vivisection arguments one by one - and destroys them. The moral, ethical, medical and scientific arguments are dealt with and Dr Coleman explains how animal experiments can produce dangerous and misleading information.

Dr Coleman explains that animal experiments are useless today and have always been useless. He goes on to discuss alternatives to animal experiments and offers readers a 10 point action plan with the aim of stopping vivisection for good. With the aid of this book you can help stop one of the world's most barbaric practices.

"A damning indictment of vivisection"
(Animals Today)

"...wonderfully clear and full of good examples"
(M.M., Glasgow)

"... an important book"
(The Vegetarian)

Price £9.95

Published by EMJ Books
Order from Publishing House, Trinity Place, Barnstaple,
Devon EX32 9HJ, England

Also available by Vernon Coleman

The Bilbury Chronicles

A young doctor arrives to begin work in the small village of Bilbury. This picturesque hamlet is home to some memorable characters who have many a tale to tell, and Vernon Coleman weaves together a superb story full of humour and anecdotes. The Bilbury books will transport you back to the days of old-fashioned, traditional village life where you never needed to lock your door, and when a helping hand was only ever a moment away. The first novel in the series.

"I am just putting pen to paper to say how very much I enjoyed The Bilbury Chronicles. I just can't wait to read the others."
(Mrs K., Cambs)

"...a real delight from cover to cover. As the first in a series it holds out the promise of entertaining things to come"
(Daily Examiner)

"The Bilbury novels are just what I've been looking for. They are a pleasure to read over and over again"
(Mrs C., Lancs)

Price £12.95

Published by Chilton Designs
Order from Publishing House, Trinity Place, Barnstaple, Devon, EX32 9HJ, England

Also available by Vernon Coleman

How To Overcome Toxic Stress
and the Twenty-First Century Blues

*'Never have I read a book that is so startlingly true. I was
dumbfounded by your wisdom. You will go down in history as
one of the truly great health reformers of our time'*
(Extracted from a letter to the author)

If you are frustrated, bored, lonely, angry, sad, tired, listless, frightened, unhappy or tearful then it is possible that you are suffering
from Toxic Stress.
      After two decades of research Dr Coleman has come up
with his own antidote to Toxic Stress which he shares with you in
this inspirational book. In order to feel well and happy again you
need to take a close look at your life and put things back in the
right order. Dr Coleman shows you how to value the worthwhile
things in life and give less time to things which matter very little at all.
The book contains hundreds of practical tips on how to cope with
the stresses and strains of daily life.

Price £9.95

Published by European Medical Journal
Order from Publishing House, Trinity Place, Barnstaple,
Devon EX32 9HJ, England

Mrs Caldicot's Cabbage War

Thelma Caldicot was married to her husband for thirty dull and boring years. The marriage could not have been described as fulfilling in any way, shape of form, but she stuck it out in her usual uncomplaining and subservient way. Then, one afternoon two police officers knocked on her door to bring her some news that was to radically change her life.

Mrs Caldicot's Cabbage War is the poignant, warm and often funny story of an ordinary woman who, after being pushed around by other people for most of her life, finally decides to stand up for herself.

"Thank you so much for Mrs Caldicot's Cabbage War.
All your books are great."
(Mrs N., Surrey)

"... quite hilarious and my sort of reading."
(Mrs C., Darwen)

"A splendid relaxing read."
(Sunday Independent)

Price £12.95

Published by Chilton Designs
Order from Publishing House, Trinity Place, Barnstaple,
Devon, EX32 9HJ, England

Also available by Vernon Coleman

The Traditional Home Doctor

Vernon Coleman has been writing about health matters for over 25 years and readers have sent him countless thousands of tips and helpful hints. These tips and hints are the sort of information that isn't going to go out of date; they are good, old-fashioned, tried-and-tested methods that have worked for people over the years.

You will find this book a great help the next time you are faced with a family health problem.

The book contains easy-to-follow tips on:

Allergies	Anorexia
Babies	Backache
Burns	Catarrh
Colds	Flu
Constipation	Cystitis
Hay Fever	High Blood Pressure
Headaches	Indigestion
Stress	Prostate Problems
Sleeplessness	Women's Problems
Tiredness	and much more

Each topic includes tips and hints for solving the problem or reducing troublesome symptoms.

Price £9.95

Published by EMJ Books
Order from Publishing House, Trinity Place, Barnstaple, Devon EX32 9HJ, England

Mindpower

Nothing has the potential to influence your health quite as much as your mind. We've all heard the phrase "you'll worry yourself to death" and scientists have now proved that it is indeed possible for your mind to at least make you ill if not actually kill you. Most doctors around the world now agree that at least 75% of all illnesses can be caused or made worse by stress and/or anxiety. But although your mind can make you ill it can also make you better and has an enormous capacity to heal and cure if only your know how to harness its extraordinary powers and make them work for you - instead of against you!

You can use Mindpower to help you deal with a range of problems including: Anxiety, Depression, Arthritis, Cancer, Asthma, Diabetes, Eczema, Headaches, Heart Disease, High Blood Pressure, Indigestion, Women's Problems, Migraine, Pain and Sleeplessness.

"Dr Coleman's Mindpower is based on an inspiring
message of hope."
(Western Morning News)

"... offers an insight into the most powerful healing agent in
the world - the power of the mind."
(Birmingham Post)

Price £9.95

Published by EMJ Books
Order from Publishing House, Trinity Place, Barnstaple,
Devon EX32 9HJ, England

Also available by Vernon Coleman

Food For Thought

Between a third and a half of all cancers may be caused by eating the wrong foods. In this bestselling book Dr Coleman explains which foods to avoid and which to eat to reduce your risk of developing cancer. He also lists foods known to be associated with a wide range of other diseases including Asthma, Gall Bladder Disease, Headaches, Heart Trouble, High Blood Pressure, Indigestion and many more.

Years of research have gone into the writing of this book which explains the facts about mad cow disease, vegetarian eating, microwaves, drinking water, food poisoning, food irradiation and additives. It contains all the information you need about vitamins, carbohydrates, fats and proteins plus a list of 20 superfoods which Dr Coleman believes can improve your health and protect you from a wide range of health problems. The book also includes a "slim-for-life" programme with 48 quick slimming tips to help you lose weight safely and permanently.

" ... a guide to healthy eating which reads like a thriller"
(The Good Book Guide)

"Dr Vernon Coleman is one of our most enlightened, trenchant and sensible dispensers of medical advice"
(The Observer)

Price £12.95

Published by EMJ Books
Order from Publishing House, Trinity Place, Barnstaple, Devon
EX32 9HJ, England

Also available by Vernon Coleman

How to Conquer Pain

If you suffer from recurrent or persistent pain then you could benefit from reading this invaluable book. It's packed with practical information designed to help you control or banish pain for good. Most exciting of all, it give detail of the many techniques you can use at home to help control and conquer your pain. It describes a small, effective and economical device you can buy which has been shown to relieve pain for 95% of arthritis sufferers. (It can also deal with many other different types of pain too.) There's a very good chance that you've got an excellent source of pain relief in your house, perhaps in your kitchen or in a cupboard somewhere. The book will tell you exactly how to use it against your pain.

"...a brilliant guide, well laid out to explain pain in general,
different treatment approaches and an excellent personal
pain management plan"
(The Good Book Guide)

"A clear and helpful handbook for pain sufferers. Perhaps
most important of all is the way in which it brings pain down
to a manageable level and gives self-help ideas for sufferers"
(The Guardian)

Price £12.95

Published by EMJ Books
Order from Publishing House, Trinity Place, Barnstaple,
Devon, EX32 9HJ, England

Also available by Vernon Coleman

Bodypower
The secret of self-healing

A new edition of the sensational book which hit the Sunday Times bestseller list and the Bookseller Top Ten Chart. This international bestseller shows you how you can harness your body's amazing powers to help you cure 9 out of 10 illnesses without seeing a doctor!
The book also covers:

- How your personality affects your health
- How to stay slim for life
- How to break bad habits
- How to relax your body and mind
- How to improve your figure
- And much much more!

"Don't miss it. Dr Coleman's theories could change your life" (Sunday Mirror)

"A marvellously succinct and simple account of how the body can heal itself without resort to drugs" (The Spectator)

"Could make stress a thing of the past" (Woman's World)

Price £9.95

Published by EMJ Books
Order from Publishing House, Trinity Place, Barnstaple, Devon EX32 9HJ, England

Also available by Vernon Coleman

Alice's Diary

Well over 16,000 delighted readers from around the world have bought this wonderful book which tells of a year in the life of a mixed tabby cat called Alice.

Alice records the year's events and disasters with great humour and insight and at long last gives us a glimpse of what it is really like to be a cat! Delightfully illustrated throughout, this book is an absolute must for animal and cat lovers everywhere.

Price £9.95 (hardback)
Published by Chilton Designs Publishers
Order from Publishing House, Trinity Place, Barnstaple,
Devon EX32 9HJ, England

Also available by Vernon Coleman

Alice's Adventures

After the publication of her first book Alice was inundated with fan mail urging her to put pen to paper once more. The result is this, her second volume of memoirs in which she shares with us another exciting and eventful year.

This delightfully illustrated book is full of the wry and witty observations on life which so delighted the readers of her first book.

Another "must" for cat lovers everywhere.
Price £9.95 (hardback)
Published by Chilton Designs Publishers
Order from Publishing House, Trinity Place, Barnstaple,
Devon EX32 9HJ, England

For a catalogue of Vernon Coleman's books
please write to:

Publishing House
Trinity Place
Barnstaple
Devon EX32 9HJ
England

Telephone	01271 328892
Fax	01271 328768

Outside the UK:

Telephone	+44 1271 328892
Fax	+44 1271 328768

Or visit our websites:

www.vernoncoleman.com
www.lookingforapresent.com
www.makeyourselfbetter.net
www.antivivisection.co.uk
www.vegetariandiet.co.uk